What they said about
Ballymun Concrete News

"It managed to be relentlessly positive against the backdrop of a tsunami of negative reporting about Ballymun, so it was a welcome antidote." – **Professor Mark Boyle**, National University of Ireland, Maynooth

"The way that the news media is going now is that, at one end of the scale, you have the Googles and all the rest of the big men but, at the other end of the scale, news is going hyper-local: even more local than it was before. To that extent, Seamus was a pioneer but, perhaps he was just a bit too early." – **Professor John Horgan**, Head of Media Studies at Dublin City University (DCU) and former Press Ombudsman

"There has been a decline in regional newspapers, both in Ireland and the UK and there is a debate about what is effectively called micro-news, small targeted newspapers. In a sense, Seamus was ahead of the game on that." – **Seamus Dooley**, Irish Secretary of National Union of Journalists (NUJ)

"I remember meeting Seamus at gigs and have been interviewed and featured in the newspaper, Ballymun Concrete news were a great to supporting Aslan and other local bands in the area." – **Christy Dignam,** Aslan

"I think local news and info is more relevant now than ever. Social Media makes information easily available but it needs a steer and Seamus is the editor and the man to do that." – **Lena Byrne**, Head of Scripting at JAM Media and formerly on the RTÉ soap, *Fair City*

"What the Ballymun Concrete News *did at time was important because Seamus was very challenging. It wasn't just soft news but about the real issues. The* Ballymun Concrete News *challenged all of us to provide the best services we could." – **Karl Heller**, Garda Chief Superintendent

IT'S WRITTEN IN
CONCRETE

Seamus Kelly

Text Copyright © Seamus Kelly, 2018
The author has asserted his moral rights

First Published in 2018 by The Manuscript Publisher
ISBN: 978-1-911442-14-1
A CIP Catalogue record for this book is available from the National Library

Typesetting, page design and layout by DocumentsandManuscripts.com
Our thanks to Oliver Franklin for proofreading assistance.

Cover design by Andy Marsh

Photos appearing in this book featured in the *Ballymun Concrete News* newspaper during the period of is publication. Copyright © Seamus Kelly unless otherwise stated.

Front cover photography by Kay Kelly
Back cover photography by Tom Farrell, Ballymun Concrete News 1

Published, printed and bound in Ireland

It's Written in Concrete

Dedication

I dedicate this book to my wife Kay, who has been my strength, my rock and soul mate for over 54 years. Without her love and support there would be no newspaper or book.

Acknowledgements

I would like to express my thanks to sponsors who generously contributed to book costs.

Sponsors

Ballymun Area office, Dublin City Council, Main Street, Ballymun

Edward MacManus of Edward MacManus Pharmacy, Civic Centre, Main Street, Ballymun

Robert Murphy, Nan's SuperValu, Main Street, Ballymun

Thomas Laverty, Thomas Laverty Pharmacy, 2C Shangan Hall, Shangan Road, Ballymun

Professor Bill Tormey, Beaumont Hospital, Trinity College Dublin and Ulster University

Also, a special thanks to Axis Arts & Community Resource Centre, Ballymun and Director, Mark O'Brien, who assisted me in the promotion of book and is generously providing the Axis 200-seat theatre for the launch and book signing.

Thank You!

Preface

In this book, I am, through my own experiences, trying to introduce a brand-new concept into reporting of news in the mainstream national and regional press, by breaking away from the traditional, negative sensationalism that affects readers all over the country and world at large. Through annoyance, frustration and anger at sections of the media's hard-hitting, negative press about the Dublin town of Ballymun, a high-rise council housing estate, I decided to do something about it as this book will show.

I could see daily, that the constant negativity was seriously impacting the 17,000-plus residents' lives. Indeed, the area had been stigmatised by the media's constant negative stories of drugs, crime and anti-social behaviour. I felt I had to do something to counteract the damaging press by producing my own newspaper, reporting positive news about Ballymun and also, getting my stories published in national and regional newspapers.

This book shows my physical and psychological determination to create my own rock-solid, positive, independent newspaper without funds or resources. It also illustrates the struggles, pain and endless hours I spent fighting to get the newspaper off the ground and keep it going with very little advertising or funds. In addition to producing positive news in the *Ballymun Concrete News*, I also had a good deal of my positive news reports published in national and regional newspapers.

In this book, I show how a struggling Ballymun community supported my efforts through fundraisers and assistance, helping the newspaper through times of difficulty.

As a freelance professional journalist, I demonstrate how national and regional newspapers took me seriously and published my Ballymun positive, by-lined news reports in their papers.

The book also delves into my personal life, to show, as young boy in early 1950s, my lack of formal education, struggling with illness, teaching myself journalism and how the experience of my early years would lead me to become a successful journalist and newspaper owner/editor.

The editorial will show that Ballymun also had been going through a massive regeneration programme, which was supposed to generate thousands of jobs and bring more private investment to the area but failed miserably to fully deliver. This €2.5b regeneration project (the largest of its size in Ireland) created, on a daily basis, hell for many thousands of residents living through the demolition and redevelopment and I had, somehow, to report news that would uplift their spirits.

The serious lack of investment in the area caused the demise of the newspaper, which was the hardest shock for me to deal with, as it carried lots of debts with it and a subsequent heart attack. The book also reflects, how all this could have been avoided had the major investment come to the area.

The first writing of the draft took only about two months, editing and rewriting took roughly about another six months.

Here I would like to thank Kay, my wife of over 52 years, for her patience and support to me in writing the book, without her love and support there would be no newspaper or book.

I would also like to thank my journalist friend, Tom Farrell, who not only has helped me with my online news pages but also, voluntarily, edited the book for me in his own time.

I would hope that you, the reader, will see the value this book is trying to convey: that there is a great need for Rock-Solid, Positive news in the modern world.

Contents

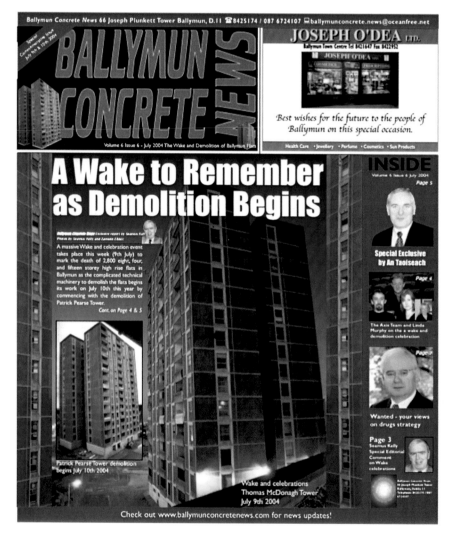

A special, commemorative issue of the *Ballymun Concrete News* newspaper.

Chapter 1

It's Time for Changes

On a warm summer's day in 1997, as I walked through Ballymun, a high-rise council estate in North Dublin, Ireland that had endured a powerful onslaught of negative media exposure for over two decades, I thought to myself, 'It's time for changes'.

A powerful desire filled me: I would somehow create my own positive-news-only newspaper for Ballymun. This was going to be the newspaper to, not only reverse that negative image but to introduce a new concept in news reporting: Positive News.

Ballymun was a huge, high-rise council housing complex. I lived among those 17,000-plus residents who had endured negative media coverage for many years. I was about to change all that. What Ballymun needed was its own independent newspaper reporting real, good news in the area, which was mostly unnoticed by national media.

It became my dream, as a national press journalist, to use my reporting skills in producing a positive newspaper for Ballymun. I had already made a small beginning, by reporting positive news stories in some of the national newspapers. However, I needed my own newspaper, which would have its own editorial control and be completely Ballymun-focused.

At the time, I lived with my wife in a three-bedroom flat on the tenth floor of the fifteen-storey Joseph Plunkett Tower, one of the famous 'seven towers' of the estate. With no money or resources, I nevertheless persevered and somehow managed to make a small start by creating a local newsletter (the newspaper would come later). Little did I realise it but, within less than two years, I would be running my own Ballymun newspaper, with high quality graphics, photographs, reporting positive news only.

Back in 1997, working as a freelance reporter for national newspapers, I was trying hard, as a journalist, to write as many positive stories as possible about Ballymun. My only equipment was a clickety-click, Remington mechanical typewriter. I would type my stories on the old machine and erase errors with bottles of Tipp-Ex. I later progressed to an electric typewriter, which had its own problems.

Having typed my story (copy), I then phoned newspaper news editors and ask if they would accept my story. I usually had about thirty seconds to convince the editor my article was worth publishing. Normally, the editor would agree to take the copy on spec and take a chance, depending on space available. The editor would say how many words he would take and then pass me over to a copy typist, who would type my copy as I read it slowly over the phone. This was a slow process: I had to read aloud to the typist, specifying exactly how it was to be written, heading, first paragraph, sentence, commas, quotes and outside quotes – exactly as on my own typed pages.

I had no internet or e-mail, just a telephone but, I was generally lucky. Most of my stories were published, mostly by-lined (with my name). However, this was just a beginning in my reporting of positive news in the national press. I remember some of the popular stories, which received wide coverage.

One of the most popular was the story of a small terrier dog called Sparky, who had lost the use of his hind legs after being hit by a car and needed a set of cart wheels to get around. Sparky was also incontinent and had to wear nappies. Luckily, he had a loving, local carer. It was a feel-good story with a happy ending. This was just one story, which ran on three different occasions in the same newspaper. There were many other positive stories I reported, which also got good coverage. However, this was not enough: I needed my own publication to cover the hundreds of stories just waiting to be told.

At the time, in 1997, I was involved with a community scheme, working on the group's newsletter. I would write news and information about the work carried out by the centre and eventually, this led to the creation of my own newsletter, which was to develop into the positive news page, reporting Ballymun's positive news. This work gave me the experience of playing around with the Microsoft Word program on the computer.

Then, using my home computer and printer donated by Edward MacManus of then Joseph O'Dea's Pharmacy, I started to practice typing stories on to the newly-designed A4 page newsletter. This was very time consuming, as it was all done in Microsoft Word on the Windows 98 operating system. Every time I created a column, text would disappear when I reached the end of the column but, after hundreds of attempts, I got it right! It was long and tedious work just creating a page. No matter how hard I tried, I could not get used to Microsoft Publisher, where the page was already created, even if it was not what I wanted. So, I found Microsoft Word easier to manage.

Now it was time to add a title to the page, which was to feature Ballymun positive news.

Quite suddenly one day, as I chatted with a friend about my newsletter, the words flowed out of my mouth, 'Ballymun Concrete News'. I was excited about the title, which was to remain over the newsletter and newspaper's lifetime. At first, the mention of the title caused some people to think that 'Concrete' referred to the concrete tower blocks in Ballymun, but it eventually sunk in that the Ballymun Concrete News meant rock-solid news. 'Rock solid positive news for the 21st century' later became the newspaper's trademark.

My judgement proved correct: the name went down very well throughout the wider community and, within a few months the words 'Concrete News' just seemed to roll off people's tongues. Within the community the prefix 'Ballymun', seemed not to matter. However, outside the area, it caught on very quickly. The concept of positive news was also something that was appreciated by my fellow journalists.

Meetings at Buswells Hotel, traditionally a media conference venue, usually included discussions on this matter. Many of my fellow journalists agreed that negative perceptions of our industry often arose from the drip-drip feed of negative news: stories that gloried in Ireland's criminal culture or told of people who were just the passive victims of disaster and horror.

I recall the first story the *Ballymun Concrete News* ran about the opening of the first new building in Ballymun in over thirty years, the Axis Arts & Community Resource Centre.

As I was an experienced professional journalist, I found it easy to cover stories just as I would for the national press. During the course of reporting national news stories over the years, I had built up a strong list of contacts and reliable sources throughout the community. These people had various areas of expertise and could be relied upon. Most importantly, they trusted me as a credible reporter. Without trustworthy and reliable sources, a journalist is all at sea. Our readers are shrewd enough to question the credibility of a story and the reporter who files it.

Having these contacts and sources helped when producing news for the *Ballymun Concrete News* and led to really good positive-news stories. The *Concrete News* newsletter became almost daily, as I would often bring out different issues within days of each other.

Being used to writing stories to tight deadlines, I would often cover and write an average story ready for copy within 2 to 3 hours. I would waste no time in contacting an editor and pitching an idea over the phone as quickly as I could. My copy would often be on the news desk in less than 4 hours. So, writing for the *Ballymun Concrete News* presented no difficulty and I was issuing a fresh newsletter within days.

Because the newsletter came out so often, people would sometimes comment to me, "But you only gave me a copy two days ago", and I would reply, "This is a new one with fresh news".

And as a result, I was in a hurry to produce as many newsletters as I could in a short space of time. A news story only has a short span of interest. There is a deadline when news is no longer fresh and that's why it needs to be rapidly delivered and distributed.

I had only an old computer and printer but no photocopier. So, I relied on local groups and agencies to support me, by photocopying the newsletter by the hundreds. Relying on local support was the only way I could distribute over several hundred copies of each issue. To begin with, I would print out the first copy of the newsletter. Then, I would bring it to one of Ballymun's local groups and ask them to photocopy it. Each local group would produce a large number of photocopies. Sometimes, my printer was unreliable. If that happened, I would save the newsletter on a floppy disk and return to the local community, ask them to print out the first page and photocopy the remainder.

Tremendous praise goes out to all the local support I had at that time, the people who assisted me in printing and photocopying the newsletter. I also had donations from the community, in the form of reams of A4 paper to help ease costs. But I wanted to expand the project.

From July 1998 to 1999, the one-page newsletter had increased to two pages and, by this time, I had local traders, businesses, agencies and local groups taking out adverts to help cover some of the everyday costs associated with its production.

Ballymun Concrete News

Volume 1 Issue 1   Created and Produced By: (c) Seamus Kelly 98 Tel: 086-8199935   Date 27th July 1998

Latest News - One Page Newsletter

Hi-Tec Art and Civic Centre For Ballymun By: Seamus Kelly.

A new cultural experience is about to hit Ballymun as a new arts and civic centre costing £2.2m out of urban development funds is expected to be built in the area within the next eighteen months. The building is to be located next to Thomas McDonagh tower which is planned for demolition early in the year 2,000.

Everything from Drama, Art, to a hi-tech recording studio and facilities will be located in the art centre. But above all local community groups are to have a managing role in the future of the centre. It is expected that a number of community groups presently working from basement flats in the area will be accommodated in the building.

According to Mr. Sean Cooke Arts and development officer of the Ballymun Partnership, the arts centre and civic offices will be linked together as one building. "The whole of the building as a centre, is a community facility, he said, and is being designed in consultation with the local residents.

I think there is a vibrant community here, I did some research in 1996 and there is a massive groundswell of arts activity in the area that's hidden," he added.

Mr. Cooke claimed this research showed at the time that eight per cent of the population of Ballymun are involved in arts and cultural activity. He said that Ballymun is at a point within the development of the whole new Ballymun, where there is an opportunity to portray this type of cultural identity. "I think a cultural perspective in relation to development is an essential part of that."

People will be involved in the management of the centre and Mr Cooke believes this will help to sustain the centre over the years. "There is a sense of ownership and people will see this as a classy hi-spec building.

It will be used in a manner, he claimed, which will facilitate the needs of the community." He indicated that they will at some point need to source funding from the arts council and central government to ensure the smooth running of the centre. "Our business plan should outline those different things and when it does we will have to take the necessary steps to find that money," he added. Mr. Cooke indicated that the Ballymun Partnerships role in this project, is to draw on the various different types of funding for the centre and "help the community take charge and develop these projects."

Editorial

=====

Welcome to the Ballymun Concrete News. This is a first for Ballymun with up to date local news on one page. Just pick a copy up from your local newsagents free of charge.

From time to time news comes up which is either too localised for Nationals or late for publication in Local papers. This is the reason for the Ballymun Concrete News, it fills the gap. There has been too much negative news hitting the daily papers over the years and it's time to put the facts straight. I've been trying to do just that over the past two years in National and Local papers.

I have received welcome recognition from the community, Gardai, and other bodies in the area for my coverage in newspapers on Ballymun issues. Hopefully this will continue, it depends on editors of National papers. I think by this stage some of them are fed up with me trying to get as much good coverage as possible.

My work has been published in Irish Independent, Irish Times, Star, Evening Herald, Irish Mirror, Sunday Independent and of course the Sunday World. Not to forget your favourite's the Northside People and Local News. **Editor: Seamus Kelly.**
Tel: 086-8199935

=========================

The first issue of *Ballymun Concrete News*, 1998.

Seamus Kelly, holding a copy of the *Ballymun Concrete News*, with some of his press cuttings on the walls of his office in his tenth-floor flat in Ballymun.

From newsletter to newspaper. Seamus checking the tabloid-format *Ballymun Concrete News* newspaper as they roll off the printing press.

Chapter 2

From Newsletter to Newspaper

The *Ballymun Concrete News* newsletter was just the beginning of what was to become a newspaper dedicated to concrete positive news. In its original format, the newsletter was a text document without photographs. This would soon change however, and I would be producing a tabloid with high quality graphics and photographs.

Although not a newspaper, the newsletter was better than nothing and reported positive news in the area, stories that other newspapers did not run. In any event, a newsletter can be just as effective as a newspaper if the news reports presented are similar in presentation and quality to those of the national press. Being a professional journalist, I had the skill to produce professional news reports.

A colleague of mine, Sean Boyne, both the news and political editor in the *Sunday World*, a major newspaper, paid quite a compliment. He said it was the only one-page newspaper in Ireland. In the first phase of its life, the *Ballymun Concrete News* newsletter produced 31 issues, running from July 1998 to 1999 as a one and then two-page newsletter. Soon after, we held a local fund-raising event in The Penthouse lounge in Ballymun. It was a tremendous night with huge attendance, which was a big uplift for me and the project.

The event was supported by local bands performing free of charge, donations from residents and local agencies. There were raffles and a local bakery provided a massive cake for the event. Even a local doctor dropped in to make a donation. We raised sufficient funds to support a graphic-designed newsletter and have it printed by litho press.

The newsletter had only been running for one year and yet, this showed the major impact it had within the community. In my view, the supporters and the Ballymun community saw this newsletter as their one-and-only, real means of communication in the area.

Yes, there were other newspapers, like the *Northside People* and the *Local News* but, they were more regional and not focused on one area. We needed our own publication and this was the best I could provide for the time being.

But I knew, from local feedback, that I was making headway. For too long people living in the area had been trapped in a negative stereotype.

After an ambitious effort to build state-of-the-art social housing in the mid-1960s, Ballymun was seen as a disaster and its people mere victims. The truth was different and this was what I sought to report: Ballymun was more an area of 'concrete people' who organised themselves and arranged the facilities and amenities that no one else would.

Having managed to raise a substantial amount of funds, I could now afford to take the newsletter to its next stage of development. I searched around to find a local graphic designer to assist me in the design of a professionally produced newsletter. (It would still be some time before I could afford a newspaper).

In the meantime, I had forged a relationship with another photojournalist and, together we agreed to form a partnership in running the newsletter. He assisted me in taking the photographs and having them scanned. We both collected the newsletters from the printers. However, after two issues, we parted company over a disagreement concerning business matters and decisions regarding taking the paper forward. But it was a dignified, mutual decision to break the partnership.

By now each newsletter was printed in a printer's shop on a litho press. I was very happy with its look – even if it was still in black and white. For the first time, photographs accompanied the text. Photography would form a very important element of the *Ballymun Concrete News* operation from then on, even if I was using a relatively simple 35mm camera.

There was, however, still a lot of work to do, as the four- and eight-page newsletters came unfolded. My wife and I would work through the night, folding and creasing them and stapling the pages together. It was monotonous work but, as the costs of folding and stapling were expensive, there was no choice but to do this ourselves.

To help offset the costs of printing and design, I secured some small advertising from local businesses, groups and agencies. The newsletter was now taking shape and I was on my way towards a real newspaper.

It was an interesting format: the banners logo on either side of the Ballymun Concrete News title was some clip art of a teddy bear selling newspapers. I had used this logo successfully in the earlier newsletters, presenting a friendly appearance. The banner also contained the headline, 'Ballymun Concrete News' together with production and circulation details for the greater Ballymun and Poppintree area, along with contact details.

The first four-page issue of the new newsletter was issued on October 1999 and ran with a story headlined, "Halloween Celebrations and Fireworks Display", reporting on planned annual fireworks to take place at the end of the month, when the skies above the towers would burst in massive displays of glittering colour.

The following issue again featured four pages, with more advertising to help cover the costs and a follow-up to the Halloween firework celebration, headed, "Firework Spectacular".

Ironically, I also reported in that issue on the regional *Northside People* new publication, under the heading, "New Dublin Newspaper for Dublin".

During this time, I never saw the *Northside People* as opposition. In fact, the then news editor, Aidan Kelly, was very supportive of my venture, giving me some editorial advice and valuable tips in reporting. The two papers were not the same. The *Northside People* had a wider focus and I had set up the *Ballymun Concrete News* with the specific aim of highlighting the positive side of Ballymun itself.

As, by now, the advertising was climbing and I needed more pages so, I increased to eight pages and more editorial. But I also had to make a major decision about the publication's future. Due to the newsletter's success and more advertising coming on board, especially at the time of the regeneration of Ballymun, I decided to change the format once again. Already producing an eight-page newsletter, a dilemma faced me: should I take a chance and produce a full-sized tabloid newspaper or stay as a newsletter? Having talked through my ideas for the newspaper with the graphic designer, I came to a decision, one which was to change the *Ballymun Concrete News* in a positive way.

Working alongside the graphic designer, Andy Marsh, in his home in Poppintree, Ballymun, we designed the pages together on his Macintosh computer, using a program called Quark XPress. Hours later, we finally came up with a front page, which we were both happy with. The graphic designer agreed to a small monthly fee, as I could not afford to employ him at a higher rate.

Even at this stage, I still did not contact a printer. Unsurprisingly, when the time came, it was a mad rush to see if I could find one who would be able to print from my designer's programme. Not long afterwards, I found myself, together with the graphic designer and another friend who had earlier worked with me in the newsletter, at a major newspaper printing press, which printed national daily and Sunday newspapers.

We waited through the early hours of the morning to see if our programme would suit their print set-up. However, our hearts sank when the printer returned with our disc in his hand. They could not print from our programme so, they sent us to a printer who would not only be able to print the newspaper but, would be with me for the lifetime of the *Ballymun Concrete News*.

Having reached an agreement over price and the minimum run of 7,500 copies per issue, he would print the newspaper on a monthly basis. I gave him the disc from which he could prepare the plates for the newspaper and within hours, the newspaper was rolling of the web press in all its glorious colours.

My next headache was how I could afford these additional monthly costs. But then, I realised that the regeneration of Ballymun would provide the necessary advertising. The community was now in the midst of vast changes.

Set up by Dublin City Council in 1997, the regeneration company, Ballymun Regeneration Ltd, had come into the community with a master plan to demolish all the flats in Ballymun and rebuild a new town. That meant that there would be additional advertising coming from builders, developers and planners.

With the funds that I managed to raise, with the help of the local community and business in the area, together with the initial secured advertising, I got the very first issue printed. As the initial advertising only covered this first issue, I had to rely on the advertisers paying in advance for the space I gave them. But this ensured that the next issue was paid for.

It took several months for a surplus to build, as each issue showed a small profit margin, covering further issues of the newspaper. I had no funding, no grants and I was self-employed at this stage. I was not entitled to government grants since I ran a private business.

Back when I had produced my first newsletter, I was in receipt of a disability benefit payment each week. However, because I had started the *Ballymun Concrete News* as a business, I had to hand back my disability book. Luckily, there was a government support in place whereby setting up my own business, I could retain some of the payments over a five-year period. Each year that I was in business, the payments would be gradually reduced. This also was a help in covering my everyday living expenses as, at this time, I did not draw a large salary.

In the early days of the first tabloid issue of the *Ballymun Concrete News* being printed, I had no transport of my own and the printer, whom I paid to print the newspaper, lived about an hour's drive away, in Ashbourne,

Co. Meath. Once more the generosity of friends proved very useful. They helped me to collect the 7,500 newspapers.

The initial production of the *Ballymun Concrete News* was 7,500 copies. This was a minimum requirement of the printer, as he used a heat-set web printing press to do the print run.

I remember the very first printed issue of the newspaper. As I had no transport and had somehow to collect and deliver 7,500 copies, I rang a friend who had access to a van and together, we collected those first new issues from the printer.

At that time, living on the tenth floor of the Joseph Plunkett Tower meant having to physically carry dozens of reams of heavy newspapers through the foyer of the building and make several trips in the lift to my home. Such trips left my fingers almost raw from carrying the bundles, which had plastic strips holding the reams together that cut into my fingers. As soon as I had managed to bundle the newspapers up ten storeys and into my flat, I fell back onto the settee exhausted. I allowed myself some rest and a cup of tea. Then it was on to sorting the papers out for delivery.

In those early days, I had no distributor. Once again, I had to physically deliver the newspapers all over Ballymun. I handed them out to everyone I passed and dropped some copies off at the local shopping centre and local business and community groups in the area. Once again, this was an exhausting business but, residents were generally enthusiastic and glad to get their copy of the paper.

Over a period of two to three years, the initial 7,500-run of newspapers, increased to 20,000, with a locally employed distributor to deliver them to the letter boxes of Ballymun homes and to various Dublin drop-off points. This was a unique journalistic achievement with a positive-news-only newspaper. No other community of social housing scheme in Ireland had seen anything like this before.

Now, the positive news through the *Ballymun Concrete News* was reaching over 100,000 readers all over Dublin. When you produce 20,000 copies, you multiply by a factor of five to get an average readership figure.

The paper had a great reception from the local community. This was a turning point in helping change the negative image of Ballymun. Now, the area not only had its own newspaper, but one which supported the positive community action there. So much of this was ignored outside yet, it took place daily. People began to organise themselves and for me, it was a privilege to be able to ensure they were not ignored.

Of course, whenever high-profile stars from the world of Hollywood and entertainment came to launch something in Ballymun, most, if not all other newspapers covered these events. These were national stories. There were also major political events in the area, such as the National Forum on Europe, where the then Taoiseach, Bertie Ahern TD opened the debate in the Axis centre with other European political representatives. This editor personally interviewed the Taoiseach on that occasion, as he had on many other of his visits to Ballymun.

I covered as many of these events as possible. At the time, armed only with a 35mm film camera donated by a friend, a Dictaphone, notebook and pen, I carried out the interviews, took the photos, transcribed tapes and notes and wrote the stories. I then edited the written stories, had the photos developed, scanned them and put them on a disk for the graphic designer, who would prepare for the printing process. Essentially, I had to be Jack-of-all-trades, as I could not afford to employ skilled personnel. I was not going to ask people to work for nothing and so, all this work fell upon me.

With all this done, I would then prepare a disc with a detailed list of all editorial for the graphic designer. This list would inform the designer where exactly, on each page and in what position, a story, image, photograph, advertisement or editorial would go.

With another graphic designer, Jamie Plummer, I would meet her once a month in the Kylemore (restaurant) on O'Connell Street, where we would have tea and I would give her the disc. Everything she needed was included on the CD. I also gave her the photograph hard copies. We would also discuss each page and how it was to be designed. She would then take the images and disc, transfer the contents to her own equipment and design the final newspaper issue.

When the graphic designer finished the paper, they would send me an Adobe PDF proof to check for errors. I would then proofread the entire newspaper, including stories, noted any changes to be made and sent it back via e-mail. When all the amendments were made, I would receive a final proof and make the decision to, what they call in the business, 'burn the disc'. This basically means save and prepare for the printer. Once the disc is burned, there can be no turning back, since it reaches the printer within hours.

The disc is then put on the printer's computer and plates prepared, then transferred to the web press and the print run commences. I often would go to the printer to watch the printing process in action. It was a wonder to observe as the huge, blank, white paper reels travelling at speed through a printing and colouring process. I marvelled at the mixture of colours being printed at each section of the web press, until it reached the end of the run, where I picked up one copy, spotless and fresh, for examination. It was a great feeling, handling the first copy that came off the line. I could not think of many things more rewarding than looking at the front page in all its glorious colour.

As web printing is a technical process, it takes time for the colours and editorial to come together, so initial copies will be messy and unusable but, as the run progresses and the printer eyes the paper carefully with each run, eventually, the paper comes together, complete in all its colour and editorial print. The type of print that this particular printer used in the printing process was called Heat Set. Wet ink was dried by driers, so it would not stain on your fingers as you handled the newspaper. This was yet another special aspect of the *Ballymun Concrete News*. Readers would have no concerns over partially dried print coming off and finding its way onto skin or clothes.

As was the case with the graphic designer, the printer was not employed staff – just paid a fee for each issue of the *Ballymun Concrete News* printed, which was once a month. However, this particular printer was special, as he believed in the *Ballymun Concrete News'* concept of producing positive news only. Some months I ran into financial problems and had to do further fund raising to keep the newspaper alive.

On one of these occasions, the printer provided me with three free issues of the newspaper. This proved to be a great help, as the printing was one of the heaviest costs. That said, the printer kept his fee at a very reasonable cost, with a print run now of 20,000 copies per month. I am forever in his debt although, he does not want any credit or mention of his good name. All I can do is say 'thank you' to him if he is reading this book. The success of my paper would not have happened without his generosity.

A print run of 20,000 copies per month meant that I could not physically distribute the newspapers on my own and without transport. I had to add another supplier to the list and pay a local distributor to deliver the newspapers to every home and premises in Ballymun, along with the drop-off points in the Dublin area. The local public library was also supportive in taking some copies and issuing copies to all other Dublin city libraries.

Without the support through fund raising and advertising from the local business, agencies, community groups and politicians, I could not keep the newspaper alive. The bulk of the expenses were covered by advertising, which covered nearly all of the costs. On some occasions, I met with local agency and business advertisers and told them of my financial problems. They all agreed to take substantial advertising over the short period, to help out and pay in advance to ensure publication of the newspaper.

With more demand for stories and an expanding operation, I could not cover all the stories myself. There were occasions when I had to use freelance reporters to supply copy and stories for the newspaper.

I also helped train aspiring young people from the local Dublin City University (DCU), at the request of the college. The campus is just a short distance from Ballymun and I came in contact with student journalists and photographers who would go on to become serious players in the mainstream media today.

On another occasion, a local politician, Fianna Fáil TD, Pat Carey, requested that I help a young man, Fiachra Ó Cionnaith, who had been studying journalism at the local DCU college and needed hands-on experience. In his early days he just needed a little encouragement and I helped by showing him how to improve his skills. In no time at all he became quite promising and I gave him some major exclusives to cover, which included interviews, such as the manager of Ireland's national soccer team of the period, Brian Kerr.

As a young journalist who had good knowledge of football, Fiachra enjoyed doing the story and made a good job out of it. Although he was just doing work experience, I paid him a fee for each story he wrote for the newspaper, with his own by-line. This same young man was to become very successful later, as he progressed into national media and actually won a Young Journalist of The Year Award. He is now political commentator with the *Irish Examiner* newspaper.

I was over the moon for him when he rang and thanked me for the training. It was very rewarding to witness a novice rise into the mainstream media. As a mentor to young reporters, I have always been extremely gratified to send the stars of the up-and-coming journalistic generation on their way.

A paid contributor wrote several features for the newspaper. Gwen McNamara – poet and author – was a great asset in helping me promote the newspaper.

I also used the services of another journalist, Sean Murphy, a reporter with *Northside People* and deputy news editor of a national tabloid newspaper. He helped me out during a difficult time when I was overloaded with work and did several stories for me.

In the very first issues of the newspaper, I also had the valuable, voluntary services of a photographer, Lena Byrne, who worked as script editor on the RTÉ soap, *Fair City*. Lena was a great asset in taking the early photographs and very supportive of the *Ballymun Concrete News*. She currently works as head script producer for CBBC Jam media.

In addition to the positive news, I introduced several column editorials on various topics. There were contributions from professional people in the community who wrote their columns regularly in the newspaper. I was careful that specialist information would be handled by people with the appropriate knowledge. I made sure the paper had plenty of expert opinion on law, business, music and medicine. We also had a *Eurolink* column, written by a journalist with knowledge of how the EU works, and a local *Garda View* column. I wanted the newspaper to, not only focus on news stories but also a few other topics that would be useful to our readers.

There was a colourful page three, which featured reviews of the local bands, stage plays, music and other theatre entertainment. Also, art and photo exhibitions that took place in the local Axis Arts & Community Resource Centre.

As editor of the *Ballymun Concrete News*, I believed that the arts and theatre would play an important role in enhancing the profile of the area. The Axis centre was now a hub where people gathered to enjoy the entertainment on offer. One could also enjoy a meal at the cafeteria and see local talent and sometimes international celebrities.

But the most important feature of the newspaper was the emphasis on positive news stories. These stories represented the real Ballymun, a place that sections of the media portrayed as being ridden with anti-social activity, drug pushing and crime. I wanted to counter this unfair caricature. By all means, crime existed in the area, along with drug pushing and anti-social behaviour. But there was also a vibrant and active community, doing Trojan work in many areas. As the editor of the *Ballymun Concrete News*, I felt it was my duty and responsibility to report on this side of the community, all too frequently neglected by the mainstream media.

How often did you hear about Ballymun as a catalyst for community activism and engagement by local people, who refused to accept their fate as hapless victims of a failed social policy? After several years of reporting on positive news, I found that these uplifting stories were much easier to find in the area than negative ones. Moreover, I would also add, from my own experience as a jobbing reporter, that this would apply in any similar area. Positive news is more rampant than the negative news that we are exposed to, on a daily basis, in the national media. These positive news stories have a very measurable effect on the morale of a local community: something I know from personal experience.

Not only is the positive news good for people's morale, there is a feel-good factor when reading or looking at the photos. It is good for the area as a whole and attracts more visitors and business. In fact, it is good for the local economy. If you are interested in investing in areas like Ballymun, it is only natural that you want to have a positive impression of the community and its people.

The negative news that bombards readers and viewers these days has been shown to be a factor in anxiety, depression and alienation, especially from the media itself. The print media existed in a different world when I set up the *Ballymun Concrete News*. Today, there are accusations of 'fake news' directed against the mainstream media and the industry is challenged by various types of social media. But I believe that a positive news service boosts the morale of its users and provides a way for today's media to save itself. Maybe they ought to give it a try?

At the time I set up the *Ballymun Concrete News*, a very audacious regeneration programme was inaugurated: high hopes existed that, for the first time, the people of the community would at last be subject to a programme that did not repeat the mistakes of the previous generation.

The agenda of the *Ballymun Concrete News*, as a means of creating a good impression, was exceptionally important at this time. During no other era, perhaps, in Ballymun's history, was it more imperative that a news reporting outlet like my newspaper was there to create an uplifting impression of the area. This was an era when the Celtic Tiger was roaring: we needed as much outside investment as we could get. If the *Ballymun Concrete News* could possibly facilitate this, I knew I was doing the right thing.

A €2.5bn regeneration programme was in place, set to demolish all the flats in Ballymun and replace them with new housing and infrastructure. This was a major upheaval for local residents. They had witnessed these flats, within which they had raised their children, being erected in the 1960s, amid high hopes that the then new flats represented a vast improvement on the inner-city squalor that had preceded them. Indeed, there had been protest marches demanding that the Lemass government provide decent social housing for working-class residents of inner Dublin.

Supposedly the definitive example of 1960s government planning, Ballymun was now to be bulldozed and bombed to the ground by explosive demolition. This was an especially important time for the paper: the *Ballymun Concrete*

News was to be a vital tool in keeping the residents informed of these developments. And we had a duty to continue to report positive events, to show there was some form of normality during the rebuilding of their town of Ballymun.

Chapter 3

Regeneration and Ballymun Concrete News

The plan was most ambitious. There were several thousand local residents who would need to be rehoused while the regeneration of Ballymun was being carried out by Ballymun Regeneration Ltd, a subsidiary company set up by Dublin Corporation.

Ciaran Murray was appointed as managing director and a voluntary Board of Directors was established.

BRL board of directors were:

> Public Representatives: Alderman Noel Ahern TD, Councillor Eamonn O'Brien
>
> Ballymun Housing Task Force: Peter Davitt, John Fitzpatrick
>
> Dublin Corporation: Brendan Kenny, Jim Barrett
>
> Ballymun Partnership: Michael Cowman
>
> Community Representatives: Patricia Kelly, Anne Keating
>
> Eastern Health Board: Pat McLoughlin
>
> Private Sector: Dermot Pierce
>
> Chairman: Dr Daniel O'Hare (DCU)
>
> Managing Director: Ciaran Murray
>
> Company Secretary: Evelyn Hanlon

The regeneration project would spare none of the old flats. A massive programme was envisioned that would demolish all of the high-rise fifteen, eight and four-storey buildings.

Although all of the residents living in the apartment blocks were to be re-homed, it was still a major transition to come to terms with: from the old Ballymun to the unknown, new town to be built. This was the end of an era. To the outside world, all of this was reported in glowing tones: the future could only be a bright one. But given the audacious nature of the plan, the community really needed an independent media voice that was not running with an agenda linked to any party or private or state body.

That's where the *Ballymun Concrete News* came in. The community needed a source of positive news at a time when, for the first time, there was a real sense that Ballymun might be transformed by the regeneration. Building works surrounding your homes on almost a daily basis can be very demoralising. So, it was important that the *Ballymun Concrete News* helped keep residents distracted for a time with its choice of news stories.

A local newspaper is not just a luxury: local people need such a media outlet. Moreover, in the context of the regeneration, the people needed someone who would report from a local perspective. Yes, there were other regional newspapers, with wider areas to focus on in addition to Ballymun. That's why the *Ballymun Concrete News* was vital in the area as it focused 100% on Ballymun news. Through *Ballymun Concrete News*, I was able to focus on one of the most important urban stories in the history of the Irish State.

The regeneration clearly raised the question of outside investment. Through the paper, I was very committed to covering whatever companies would invest in the community and what employment opportunities they would provide.

With the promise of a €300 million shopping centre, there was great expectation that the *Ballymun Concrete News* would benefit from the retail to be housed in the centre, in addition to the thousands of jobs that would also be created. I personally sought to benefit my newspaper business from whatever investment naturally followed on. Unfortunately, however, even now the shopping centre has failed to materialise. Go to today's estate and the old 1970s shopping centre is still an empty precinct, with businesses boarded up and empty: a depressing sight and something that angers the locals.

By right, the shopping centre should exist as a hub for the community. My newspaper's future was reliant on the advertising revenue from the proposed shopping centre, together with a business park, which also failed to materialise. Looking back, what was especially frustrating was the fact that the shopping centre was given the green light to go ahead but then, disputes flared between the developer and Dublin City Council. So Ballymun never received what was promised.

Further new plans were drawn up to build the shopping centre and once again, this plan received planning permission, However, at the height of the Celtic Tiger boom, a government plan to introduce a metro rail service to pass through Ballymun, beginning in Dublin Airport, was dropped and the shopping centre plans were also scrapped. The reason for the cancellation was that it would not be viable for new retail development without the metro travelling through Ballymun.

One by one, local traders have left the centre, leaving the shopping mall a deserted centre. Today, at the time of writing, plans are in place to demolish the shopping centre once last trader has left.

An empty shopping centre was a shocking loss to the community that had previously used it as a hub, where locals would meet and socialise. There had also been plans for a business and technological park but again, these came to nothing. The fact that fresh investment never came about also spelt the end of the *Ballymun Concrete News* newspaper. There was simply no way I could survive without secure advertising.

In theory, Ballymun was blessed by the regeneration plans. To ensure investment came to the area, tax incentives were introduced to attract new business. However, in practice, only a small number of retail units were ever opened.

I tried to secure alternative advertising to survive but it was hopeless. So, with a sad heart I had to let the business go. The folding up of the *Ballymun Concrete News* also left me carrying a number of financial debts. This left both me and my fellow residents in a precarious position.

Certainly, the flats complex had been demolished and replaced with new housing, new infrastructure and roads and neighbourhood centres. However, something vitally important had failed to materialise: the massive investment that could certainly have turned the community around.

Many families were re-housed in new homes throughout the area. New parks were developed and a new Ballymun Civic Centre was built. The Axis centre has certainly benefited the community. However, although this was the first building to be developed in the new Ballymun, Axis was not part of the regeneration process, having been funded by the EU, government local planning development funds and arts funding.

I remember the promised regeneration project being an exciting era. As proprietor and editor of the *Ballymun Concrete News*, I had great plans and hopes to develop and expand the newspaper as soon as the projected investment came to the area. To that end, I took out an overdraft and acquired loans from the bank, in order to keep the *Ballymun Concrete News* going and increase the circulation until that development was secure. Even the local bank could see that my business plan for the *Ballymun Concrete News* was a good investment. So, I had no problem getting credit to cover my overheads. Sadly, the taking out of these loans and overdraft would prove to be damaging in the longer term, when the said investment failed to materialise. Nevertheless, I kept the newspaper going for as long as I possibly could. Alas, that only led to more financial difficulties for me.

The *Ballymun Concrete News* stories provided the readership with a comfort in the face of demolition and the clouds of dust billowing up from the nearby building works. The incessant noise from the operation was a daily source of headache and annoyance. Meanwhile, I sought to present a more upbeat picture. The local residents needed cheering up and especially with the destruction of the iconic roundabout in the centre of the old estate. From the point of view of the *Ballymun Concrete News*, it was important to present an alternative perspective. People needed to know there was a degree of sanity in the area. But redirecting folks' attention towards the positive was a challenge. Like any other resident, I too was affected by the ongoing regeneration works. Most of the time, the whole estate was flooded with heavy machinery, along with the noise of drilling.

When a regeneration of this magnitude takes place, fundamentally altering the lives of residents living in the area, the process is guaranteed to be a punishing one and it has lasted for over fourteen years to date. There I was, promoting the area through my newspaper and yet, I was the first local business to go to the wall. In many ways, what happened to the *Ballymun Concrete News* was symbolic of the wider failure to bring about a successful process of regeneration, wherein the life Ballymun could have been turned around.

After eight years doing my best to turn around the image of the community through a positive news service, I was forced to let go. The *Ballymun Concrete News* was brought down by the wider failure of the regeneration itself. This was one of the worst blows I ever received as a veteran reporter. The folding of my paper really broke me up.

Once it was clear that the shopping centre was a non-runner, I would lose everything I had built up over those eight years. In addition to this, I was deeply annoyed by the fact that the local residents would not have their promised shopping centre. This was vital to turning the community around and should have been among the top priorities of the regeneration. These days, they can still walk through an empty shell, constantly reminded of promises made and promises broken.

On a personal level, I was heartbroken that I could no longer report the positive news, which helped Ballymun gain its pride once again. I had simultaneously lost my business and also accumulated serious debts in the process. I had borrowed on the strength of private investment coming to the area and took big chances and risks. The failure of the shopping centre, for me, was a personal disaster. It would take me several years to repay the bank and get myself back together again.

However, the journalistic 'fire' continues to burn within me. In recent years I have set up several Facebook pages including Ballymun Concrete News, Dublin Concrete News and Ballymun Concrete News Photo Archives. I retain my passion for news reporting and a belief in the importance of positive news. There is no income in administering these news pages but, at least I am able to continue promoting positive news on Facebook. The page is run just like a professional newspaper, with real news reports, thanks to a loyal friend and journalist who covers the stories and takes photos for me.

Nowadays, we live in a society deluged by negative media. Thus, we need an alternative media to balance the good and bad news. It is important that people are exposed to positive news, to create a feel-good factor.

When I wake up each morning and face the daily headlines, I feel a little depressed when I hear of the onslaught of another murder, rape, or war in other parts of the world. Studies have shown that I am not the only one. Recent academic research has proved that a steady avalanche of horrible and soul-crushing stories really does impact in a negative way on the psychological health of people, producing anxiety, depression and low morale.

That said, I don't argue against the importance of reporting these stories. We need to keep informed about crime and geopolitics. However, I believe there is a need to present these stories in a more balanced and sensitive manner. They should not be ignored but, there are ways to report them in a context where some element of hope or positivism is also present.

Sensationalism helps sell newspapers and negative headlines and photos are aimed to attract readers, at least in the short term. However, from my own perspective, as a long-term reporter who has written for many publications, I don't believe in promoting gory photos of blood-stained bodies or other upsetting negative images on the front page. I know from the popular reaction to such stories as Sparky the paralysed terrier dog, (see *Chapter 16*) and the woman who took him in and nurtured him, that the reader is more likely to click with a hopeful, upbeat story.

In the case of the *Ballymun Concrete News*, when we were presented with a tragic or negative subject matter, I managed to put a positive angle to the story. It would take another book to explain the ways in which the negative stories can be promoted in a very positive style, so as not to upset readers or victims. But this, I believe, is something we in the media, need to discuss.

It is always the victims of crime or war who suffer the pain of reading and seeing the negative photos and news stories. Who wants to read negative news about a family friend, who has been attacked or murdered, presented in a very insensitive manner? I would advise editors to always keep this in mind: there are the victims to be considered when presenting the news. Do these people, or their families, want to be the victims again of horror and disaster?

Based on my own experience, positive news reporting can help promote good will among people in addition to the feel-good factor. This is what I have been doing in the *Ballymun Concrete News* newspaper and national press reporting. Positive news stories can help repair the reputation of the news industry at a time when journalists are often distrusted or seen as unethical.

Onlookers witness the demolition launch at Patrick Pearse
Tower, Ballymun, 2004.

Minister Noel Ahern TD (Fianna Fáil) and Ciaran Murray of Ballymun
Regeneration Ltd at Thomas MacDonagh Tower, to announce the demolitions of
the flats complex, 2004.

Newly erected traffic junction at Thomas Clarke Tower, Ballymun.

Entrance to the Ballymun Shopping Centre as it exists today, in 2018.

Chapter 4

My Work in the National Press

My work with the *Ballymun Concrete News* was preceded by several years writing with the national press. Working as freelance journalist, I established the positive news ethos that I would continue during my time writing about Ballymun.

Being upset with the image created by generally negative headlines about Ballymun, I decided to ring around news editors and inform them that I would be submitting copy with a positive news slant. I knew I could do this because I lived in Plunkett Tower for many years and had the right contacts to get those stories out. In general, I got a very good reception. For the most part they loved stories about the Ballymun area. A story about the community was always likely to be taken up by a given editor as, mostly, news stories had created a picture of an urban disaster area, whose population were largely victims of a failed project in social housing.

My first by-lined article, which ran in the *Irish Star*, headlined, "Santa Will Sleigh Them", was well received. This was a Christmas story about a couple of horses dressed as reindeer, pulling the fat, red-suited figure of Santa Claus in a makeshift sleigh into the local shopping centre, to the thrill of the young children.

At that time, I was focused on getting as many stories published in the national and local newspapers as possible, even if I was a bit of a late-comer to journalism. The *Ballymun Concrete News* was still a few years in the future. But what I did during these next few years was to provide me with excellent preparation. I got more and more of my stories published in both the local and national press. From the outset, positive news was my agenda.

It was wonderful to see my articles in print and to show them to friends in the local community. There is a special kind of pride that comes with seeing your writing go out to thousands of readers, your story exposed to the nation.

When I needed positive news stories, I was well able to get them. There was never a shortage of good news. With over one hundred groups active in Ballymun at that time, there were plenty of people ready with stories that the readers would find uplifting. One early example was the campaign against drug dealers.

During 1997, there was a drugs problem in the Ballymun area and it had almost reached epidemic proportions. The community was seriously affected, with the problem reaching to people's hall doors. At the time, the flats were very exposed, with no security doors to keep drug pushers and users out of the blocks. The stairwells leading up to each floor were constantly used for shooting up and selling drugs. But then, the local residents decided enough was enough and took action.

Parents of young children were scared that their kids might pick up contaminated syringes, which users discarded in the green and play areas around the flats. A number of the resident's mothers, fathers and neighbours sprang into action by forming anti-drugs groups and barricading the entrances to the flats, which kept pushers and users at bay.

The anti-drug residents were really well organised. It only took a short time until all the flats in the area were protected by the residents, who then set up a round-the-clock, peaceful 24-hour vigil. This was 'people power' at its most progressive and, sure enough, the efforts of ordinary folk made the activities of the users and pushers all but impossible.

One story that I was particularly pleased with ran in the then *Evening Herald* with the headline, "Drugs, Community Winning the Fight". This was an account of how the local Ballymun community reacted against the parasites who distributed deadly drugs to young people. Every segment of Ballymun was represented in this courageous stand against the drug pushers. No violence was used during this campaign. Since criminals profited from the sale and distribution of these illegal chemicals, anyone trying to enter the building, not known to residents or living in the block, would be barred from entering.

Night-time was tough for the drug watches. Local people, who were determined to prevent Ballymun's youth from falling victim, would be out in the chilly evening with just flasks of tea or maybe a cup of soup. They would patiently stand round a blazing fire lit from wood pallets in an old oil barrel. Each night, I would patrol these areas, visiting the drug watches and getting their individual stories for the newspapers. They were always helpful and many times, I shared the heat of the flames.

There was a lot of enthusiasm for such stories. I was proud to be reporting their bravery. The actions of these people were taken up in the media and the outside perception of the area's image was becoming more positive. Increasingly, Ballymun was being seen more than just an estate inhabited by victims. I was keen that outsiders knew that locals could sort out the problems and solve them on their own terms.

But drug dealing was not unique to Ballymun. This was an era when the city was awash with illegal drugs. Of course, each neighbourhood had its own way of fighting the epidemic. Yet, I also witnessed the drug dealing with my own eyes. I saw the effects it had on my own community. Naturally, this reinforced my determination to write articles that showed the local community fighting back.

I was at an advantage for the simple reason that I knew all the local sources, including the Gardaí. On that point, the Ballymun Gardaí under the supervision of Garda Sergeant Karl Heller (now retired Chief Superintendent at Harcourt Square) were very supportive of the drug watches and visited the watches on their day and night patrols. Years later, I would learn from Karl Heller that the guards were always watching out for my safety whenever I did my night rounds alone, gathering stories from the drug watch residents.

The local council also assisted the drug watches by providing mobile phones, in the event they needed assistance at a later stage. During the campaign, there were often very powerful scenes, with huge crowds massing in the local shopping centre car park, organising protest marches against known dealers in the area.

I remember one story I reported in *The Star* newspaper about the comedian Brendan O'Carroll, who was among the supporters at one of these major rallies. This, of course, added more weight to the story as Brendan was and remains a high-profile comedian (known the world over as Mrs Brown in *Mrs Brown's Boys*, his hit situation comedy).

My reporting ethos was important to the image of Ballymun. If it had not been present, the negative stereotype would have remained.

But the anti-drugs campaign was by no means the only story that *Ballymun Concrete News* worked on. There were stories which were of human interest: sad stories, happy stories and exciting events like rock festivals, theatrical productions and family fun days.

If the *Ballymun Concrete News* achieved anything, it was to take issue with the prejudiced view of an estate whose people had, over many decades, shown an extraordinary resilience, even if the 'status quo' was to write them off. I believe it's still important to report all these pro-active events happening in the community, especially if they have been neglected by the mainstream media. Ballymun's people deserve better than the simplistic narrative of victimhood.

If a news editor lived in a particular area, would he or she be happy to be continuously barraged within their own neighbourhood with a tide of negative news? What I have tried to do in my own newspaper and press work (and still try), is to give my own area a really good image, to represent it as a place you would like to live. What positive news is all about is helping local communities see the good in their own neighbourhood and encouraging locals to get involved in positive activities.

While negative stories can result in a copycat syndrome, this can also apply to positive stories. Encouraged by positive and optimistic reportage, readers can be encouraged not be feel demoralised. They can feel empowered and understand that they do have it within them to make real changes. This is something I passionately believe: a good journalist has a sense of vocation and a duty of care towards readers.

Consider my reporting of the anti-drugs campaign. Think of the results: a reduction in criminal acts, safer roads, safer communities, encouragement of locals to get out and make real, concrete changes to Ballymun and the lives of the people there. This can only help the growth of local communities and benefit themselves and neighbours.

When business and investors are looking for an area to invest, where some young couple are looking for a home to purchase, where someone wants to sell their property, then it's important the area has a positive label. Investors, first-time buyers and any other business is going to be put off when the media represents the area as a scourge.

But in this day and age, my emphasis on positive reporting just needs a little encouragement from the mainstream. To that end, I believe it is high time for a serious rethink in media circles. As I have tried to do with *Ballymun Concrete News*, let us have more positive coverage and use our reports as a means of helping others and our communities.

I do believe this is borne out by my own experience, working as a freelance journalist and being a member of the National Union of Journalist (NUJ) Dublin Freelance branch. Based on conversations with other members and some officials, I believe there is strong support for this way of news reporting in the mass media.

I also speak from personal experience. Once a month, I used to attend the freelance branch meeting and when it was over, we would all head over to the Buswells Hotel bar for the real meeting (as we would often say). I would distribute the latest issue of my newspaper to the group. The *Ballymun Concrete News* was of interest to my colleagues and several of the other journalists would end up discussing my newspaper.

They were taken aback and surprised by its colourful, graphic content, especially given my ability to get 20,000 copies to readers in Ballymun and the greater Dublin area. They were also impressed with *Ballymun Concrete News'* style of reporting positive news and not the usual unpleasant, graphic headlines most of us were familiar with. Given the encouragement I got from fellow NUJ members about the *Ballymun Concrete News*, I am more optimistic that change will come and more of the media will copy my style of news reporting.

This is what the Irish Secretary of the NUJ, Seamus Dooley said of the *Ballymun Concrete News* newspaper in a report carried on my news pages, "The *Ballymun Concrete News* is a micro news service, which is ahead of its time."

His analysis was repeated by a number of media academics, including Professor John Horgan, Head of Media Studies at Dublin City University (DCU) and an ex-ombudsman. Prof Horgan also commented favourably about the *Ballymun Concrete News* as a positive news service in the community. He had this to say about the paper:

> *"The way that the news media is going now is that, at one end of the scale, you have the Googles and all the rest of the big men but, at the other end of the scale, news is going hyper-local: even more local than it was before. To that extent, Seamus was a pioneer but, perhaps he was just a bit too early."*

These comments, from eminent news academics, were a source of praise and encouragement to me. Feeling vindicated by Seamus Dooley and John Horgan's assessments of the paper, I hope that I will somehow encourage other members of the media to adopt this style of reporting.

There are many examples of negative journalism, which may entail incorrect reporting and could possibly be misleading to the reader. Consider the example of some so-called scientist or medical expert issuing dire warnings about what is damaging to our health. These are often extracts copied from medical journals or publications and reported as news items. This is not only irresponsible journalism but also, in most cases, deliberately negative news, which can be very disturbing for readers. Given the fact that the industry is challenged by falling revenues and declining sales in many cases, it is unsurprising that much of the public has a generally cynical view of the media and are voting with their feet.

In my own *Ballymun Concrete News* newspaper, I preferred to use column writers on health and other professions. It is not my role to tell readers what is bad for their health or what might KILL them. In many cases these 'findings' are invalidated within months, at most. It seems as though anything can destroy your heath these days. Official guidelines are changing all the time! Such reporting is best left to the experts.

As an editor, I have always made a point of not alarming my readers with such rubbish. Many times, supposedly 'respectable' mainstream media outlets have run with alarmist stories about health dangers that are overturned months or years later. This careless and sloppy way of reporting something very important undermines the job of the journalist and his/her credibility. I did have a medical column writer in the *Ballymun Concrete News*, an expert who could give simple advice on a number of first aid and general, everyday health concerns like colds, flu and children's measles, etc.

Newspapers' first responsibility is to their readers, to report the facts, not conjecture or opinion (unless it's the editor's comment column). Steer clear of copying information from health and medical journals and lazily recycling theories and speculation as hard news.

Given this failure by today's journalism, it is little wonder that newspaper sales are dropping. Contrary to what many assume, it's not all down to the internet.

With regard to issues of a professional nature – such as legal advice, music reviews, business and financial advice, Europe and EU, Gardaí (police) review – I have always had professional experts writing for me.

It is useless to take quotes and information from various other periodicals and reports, then run such articles as solid news. Certainly, use these reports as leads to cover and report independently on news stories or features. Government reports on various issues and other commissioned reports again, treat as leads and not verified, independent news. Such reports are not gospel, so it's the responsibility of media to investigate. Scepticism is the mark of a good reporter.

Aspiring journalists do not need to be afraid of editors. They need your skills as a reporter, with good sources and contacts. Without you, they would have no news and possibly no job. Over the years writing in the national press, I always made a point of developing a good working relationship with the news editors, which always proved beneficial. I never pushed them over payments. Some journalists have problems getting paid on time and sometimes have to wait for long periods.

On most occasions, once my story was published, I would ring the next day, telling the editor that it had run on a particular page under the appropriate headline. I would then ask how much payment would be forthcoming. He or she would then quote me the amount that I was owed and I would never argue.

I often discussed this at NUJ freelance branch meetings, when other journalists said they were having problems getting paid. They were more than surprised I had this arrangement and that I got paid quickly. I don't know if they followed my advice to form better relations with their news editors.

The only payment delays I experienced were when I just submitted an invoice to accounts without informing the editor first. I believe it worked so well for me in that I rang the editor the day after publication, so he or she could sign off the payment immediately. Other journalists will probably recognise this problem of failing to receive payment in reasonable time. I make this point to emphasise the difficulties freelance journalists experience while waiting for their well-earned payment for published work.

As I dealt regularly with news editors, we usually had a short, friendly exchange and then discussed copy of the work. I had a lot of my copy accepted and most of this was published within a day or two, depending on the story's deadline. I supplied my copies to nearly all the national newspapers. These included: *Sunday World*, *Star*, *Irish Independent*, *Irish Mirror* (then the *Evening Herald*) and the odd other British tabloid, like the *Sunday People*.

I remember one really friendly news editor (now deceased) with the *Irish Mirror*. He jokingly said to me, "Why are you giving the *Sunday World* the best human-interest stories?"

I told him it was just the way it worked out, as I had a routine of alternating sending copy to different publications. One week, I would send to the *Irish Mirror*, next time, the *Sunday World*. The *Sunday World* was convenient as, if I submitted a news feature, it would be printed midweek, so I would know in advance if it would actually run.

However, once I had set up my own newspaper, my national press work dwindled. Committed to getting out positive news for the *Ballymun Concrete News*, I just did not have time to do work for both. Having said that, I did submit the odd article, especially if my own newspaper was running the same story. In that situation, I would only have to cover and write the story once.

Looking back, I really enjoyed my time working alongside news editors and colleagues in the national and local press. I was able to interact with talented and generous editors and reporters at all times. Moreover, these editors also relied on my expertise in the Ballymun community. I would often get a phone call from an editor, either looking for information about a local story or requesting me to cover one. They knew that I was uniquely placed in the community and had a wide range of reliable contacts.

I remember one story especially. I got a call one day, at a time when I was really busy on my own publication, from the news editor of the *Irish Mirror*. He asked me to cover a major story where a young child had been burned to death in a flat in Ballymun. At first, I declined, as it was a tragic story and, in addition, I was very tied up with my own work for the *Ballymun Concrete News*. But then I had a change of heart. The editor told me that a newspaper had run that story but, they had got the information wrong and wanted me to put the record straight. When it was put to me like that, I felt honoured that they trusted me to correct the inaccurate reporting of a major story.

It transpired that an evening newspaper had run its report alleging that the mother of the child was not at home at the time of the fire. Naturally, this was very hurtful to the grieving family of the child. The editor also told me that the newspaper had printed a clarification on this report that day.

I made a few enquiries and phoned the parents of the mother of the child and arranged a meeting with them. After the lengthy interview, I carried out other investigations and spoke with a Garda Inspector in Ballymun, to confirm that the mother was at home at the time of the fire. I told the editor I had the story and was in process of writing copy. After this, he sent out a photographer to take photos. Following this, however, there were to be some surprising developments.

As it was very late that evening, I had not yet sent copy to *Irish Mirror* and the following morning, there was a knock at my door. Standing on my doorstep was the mother of the deceased child. Immediately she asked me to not run with the story. I asked why and she told me that her solicitor would be taking legal action against the newspaper. Naturally, I was flabbergasted at this. I had all the details ready to send to my editor in Belfast. So, I asked the young mother if I could ring my editor in Belfast, while she waited in my sitting room and she agreed.

When I rang him and let him know what the problem was, he advised me to ask the young woman if I could speak to her solicitor and see if he would allow my copy to run. She agreed and gave me the appropriate phone number, which I telephoned straight away. He spoke with me for some time while I explained what I had discovered to be the real facts of this tragic story to be. Thus, he asked me to facsimile (fax) a copy to him. This was a most unusual practice: normally, we reporters do not show copy to anyone before print. However, as I could not possibly let such an important story go, I agreed and faxed the copy to his office in Belfast.

After a short time, he spoke to me again and was quite satisfied with the article – so off went my story to the *Irish Mirror*. Wow, what a relief! The story ran in the end. It was well worth the phone call to the solicitor as the story benefited both the bereaved mother and her family.

Next day, my by-lined report ran across a two-page spread in the *Irish Mirror*. This was not a negative story. Yes, it was a sad human-interest story but one that revealed the true facts. Namely, that the mother of the dead child had been in the home at the time of the fire. Furthermore, that she and neighbour tried but failed to rescue the child who died in the fire.

The fact that my *Irish Mirror* report helped the young mother clear her name after the incorrect facts were reported in another newspaper was very satisfying, and I felt that I was working for the public good as a journalist.

This is an aspect of the job which sometimes is not easy. It is inevitable that, sooner or later, the journalist will encounter highly emotive stories. The work is more than just doing interviews and writing up copy: you actually get to feel the story and the people connected with that story. Some journalists not only have they to cover and report but somehow, we have to distance ourselves from the emotions bound up with the event. That is not always easy.

The national and local press has run quite a few emotionally wrenching stories by me. Among them, is the inspiring story of a model who had been told by her doctors that she would never walk again. This story ran on three different occasions: in the *Sunday World* and a national Sunday newspaper.

As I have been keen to report, Ballymun was a community that was full of good stories and I had no shortage of such positive, rock-solid accounts to fill each monthly issue. However, I was sometimes challenged by the shortage of advertisements. Now and then, an issue could not run as there was not enough advertising to cover the costs.

Despite it all, having the *Ballymun Concrete News* newspaper was a source of comfort, knowing what I had achieved even without a full education. In the 1950s I left school at the age of fourteen. From there, I started my long journey towards journalism and the *Ballymun Concrete News*.

PRAYERS FOR DRUG WATCH

SEAMUS KELLY

A SILVER Jubilee Mass was being celebrated in Sillogue Parish in Ballymun yesterday, while just across the road residents were continuing their round-the-clock anti-drug vigil.

Only last week comedian Brendan O'Carroll led an anti-drugs rally in the area.

Sillogue Road is celebrating 25 years as a parish, and the Mass is the beginning of their week long celebration. The community, battling against drug dealing, has also found time for their church and parish.

Retired auxiliary Bishop, Jim Kavanagh concelebrated the Mass.

Fine Gael TD Mary Flaherty and colleague Brendan Brady were among the congregation which also included Dublin Corporation representatives.

During the offertory of the Mass, candles were lit as a sign of hope for a brighter future for Ballymun.

Speaking from the pulpit Mark Kelly of Sillogue Parish said: "Groups like Drug Watch show people taking pride in their own areas. This is where we can see the beginning of togetherness again through this we hope we see fresh growth in our community," he added.

DAILY STAR Tuesday May 20^ '97

Time Out For Ballymun Drugwatch

New Finglas Link Road

Fingal County Council has proposed the construction of a link road between Jamestown Road and St Margaret's Road in Finglas.

BRENDAN JOINS THE BATTLE TO BEAT DRUGS

March on homes after the meeting

BAWDY Brendan O'Carroll braved lashing rain this week to wage a personal war on drugs.

The comic addressed a rally of residents in Ballymun in his crusade to rid the capital and the country of the scourge of heroin.

The star of The Courier has already spoken to children in 30 schools around the country about the dangers of drugs.

And on Monday night in Ballymun, he started his speech by cracking a couple of typically witty comments.

SEAMUS KELLY

Crowd

But he quickly turned serious, telling the crowd that that drugs do not recognise any age boundaries.

He congratulated the people of Ballymun for turning out, and wished them the best of luck in their efforts to clean up their community.

"I know your efforts are going to be fruitful," he said.

And he advised everyone to be aware of what was going on in the flats.

"Walk down to your landing, to your left and right, make sure you know what's going on in your building," he said.

"Look after your front door, your landing. Look after your kids, and let the Gardaí do the rest," Brendan added.

The rally was organised by Ballymun Residents Against Drugs and speakers from the organisation also addressed the crowd.

Pushing

An garda looked on as they claimed that some of the pushers had signed statements agreeing not to take part in any further drug pushing.

And they said that they were not against drug addicts themselves, and invited them to come forward to get help.

A march took place after the meeting in some shaped journey time.

And one top drugs resident became involved in a heated exchange with the pushers.

An around-the-clock vigil has been taking place in Ballymun for the past three months in a bid to rid the area of drugs.

O'CARROLL: Watch out

Reports by Seamus Kelly on anti-drugs campaigns in Dublin that appeared in national and regional press (*Star* and *Northside People* newspapers), 1997.

The story of Sparky, a terrier who needed wheels and nappies to get around, was reported on by Seamus Kelly and appeared in the *Sunday World*, *Irish Mirror* and *Northside People* newspapers, 1998/99.

A selection of press cuttings (*Star* and *Sunday Mirror*) from Seamus Kelly's time reporting for national and regional newspapers.

Chapter 5

My Life

My involvement with the print media started early, to say the least! At the tender age of three years old, I could read the newspaper. My mother often told her friends and neighbours about my reading skills.

However, my memories are vague. I do recall looking at the banner of the newspaper. The logo of the *Evening Press*, a sadly long-departed paper, was fascinating to me. Ironically, looking back, this logo turned out to be not unlike my own newspaper's banner, even if the background colour of mine is black, unlike the *Evening Press*, which was pink, or near enough to pink.

By around the age of ten, before heading off to school at 9 am, I worked with the milkman, delivering milk in my native Cabra West, Dublin. It was tough going. I would rise at 3.30am, Monday to Friday and meet the milkman in the darkness at 4 am, having walked over a mile to get there. I then worked from a horse and cart milk float, and helped the milkman deliver freezing cold, clear glass, milk-filled bottles throughout the area.

Carrying several pint bottles in between fingers of each hand and under my armpits, I would begin to drop them at the doorstep of each house. I would often go to school directly after my milk round. Sometimes, I arrived there soaking wet from being caught in the rain. Back then, young boys had to grow up very quickly and times were hard. Every penny counted, including my half-crown (12-and-half pence today) wage.

I had already had a serious health crisis in 1951, during my earlier childhood (at 7 years old). I developed tonsillitis and had to go into hospital to have them surgically removed – they took out your tonsils in those days when you had tonsillitis. However, something happened then that changed my life: I almost died on the operating table.

My mother told me of this afterwards. My heart stopped during the operation and, although I lived to tell the tale, I was left with a few problems. It later transpired I had a heart condition called a heart murmur and rheumatics. She went on to tell me that the hospital arranged to dress me in new clothes and send me to Linden Convalescent Home, Blackrock, Co Dublin. This was quite a distance from where I lived in Cabra West. Taking around an hour and a half on the buses, it was difficult for my mother and father or family to visit me regularly.

Over the next two years, I would be mostly bedridden. But the experience wasn't all bad as, when I began to recover, we would play on the swings in the playground and take long walks through the meadows in Linden's vast woodland.

I was in a large ward (and it would have seemed especially big to a seven-year-old) but, there were a number of other boys on the ward with more serious heart problems than me. I made great friends with some of them but, unlike me, most of them sadly didn't survive. I suppose, I was the lucky one. I have often wondered why I did not die like the other boys; perhaps I lived for a purpose?

I must admit, I was treated very well in Linden. The nurses were terrific and we had a ward prefect who kept an eye on us at night. Some of the religious nuns (sisters) were quite stern. You had to behave yourself. Although I was very sick, I made a steady recovery and I did enjoy my time in Linden.

While convalescing, I could not go to school so, I missed a number of terms and just about received basic education. There was a classroom for some of the children but, I was not well enough to attend it.

Once I was home again and fully recovered, my mother took me to the national primary school, just up the road from our house in Cabra West. I remember speaking with the head teacher and him telling me that I would have to go to remedial class. I resented going there, as I seemed to understand that it was a class for children with learning difficulties. However, I adapted and settled in very well, and tried to catch up. I was not very good at Maths or History but was very good at writing and English. I always found writing on paper very relaxing; perhaps this was a clue to my future as a journalist?

As I said earlier, at ten, I got a job working with a milkman. But unfortunately, I got caught in the rain and ended up in Linden again. Luckily, this time I was older and strong enough to recover more quickly. Again, I was put into a remedial class but, being put there did not bother me this time. I was eleven now and only in third class in primary education. I managed to stay in school until I was fourteen and only attained fourth class, just missing fifth.

In the Ireland of the early fifties, most children left school as soon as possible in order to get jobs. This was especially the case with boys who wanted to be big men, like their fathers. I was no different and got, in 1959, my first real job working as a messenger boy for a butcher, delivering meat to local houses. After a year, however, I got the sack for feeding local dogs: they were always following me on my trusty messenger boy's bike, with its huge basket filled with fresh meat at the handle bars.

When I got a new job with a messenger service in Dublin City Centre, my journey on the road towards journalism began. This new position, involved collecting copy (written story) from journalists and delivering it to the offices of national newspapers. I would be sent on a bicycle to the nearby Four Courts and other courts where reporters covered cases and collected their stories from them (called copy). I would also collect journalists copy from other major events centres, where news stories were being covered.

Other areas where the journalists worked included the RDS, where the Dublin Horse Show was a national event and I would also collect the reporters' copies for delivery to the press offices. This was an important job as the copy was for publication in the daytime or evening newspaper. I had the sole responsibility to ensure its safe arrival at the newspapers office. I would deliver some reporters' copy to the *Mail* evening newspaper in Parliament Street. Other copy went to national newspapers, the *Irish Press*, Burgh Quay and the *Irish Independent* offices in Middle Abbey Street.

This gave me the chance to see the inside of, not only the mail room but also, the printing room. I remember, as if it were yesterday, being inside the Irish Independent printing room, seeing those typesetters preparing their printing blocks for print. These were heavy equipment with reverse type letters which, when printed on newspaper, came the right way up.

For me, it was such an exciting feeling being around the print and mail room, which was near the reporters and news room. Like my early reading and love of English, perhaps this was another sign for my future as a journalist. Not only could I smell the printing room aroma but, I sensed a belonging and the adrenalin flowing through my body: a foretaste of what I would be doing fifty years later.

I never really settled down in those years, going from job to job. However, I worked as an apprentice glazier, a shunter on the railway, factory hand, manager of a retail newsagents, storeman and in many other professions, including a job in a hospital, looking after young people with addiction problems.

As I didn't have much of an education and, by the mid-sixties, a married man with responsibilities, I decided to further my education. But in those days, there was no funding for adults wanting to do that. So, week after week, I took education grinds, which I paid for from my daily work.

It wasn't until the mid-1970s that I turned my hand to writing seriously. I submitted an article to *The Way* journal, a Jesuit religious magazine for which I received my first payment of forty pounds. However, while it was a great experience, I didn't think then that I would ever be running my own newspaper.

During the early eighties I suddenly developed a new problem. I was afflicted by a bad case of agoraphobia. My own home became a prison for more than eight years.

Agoraphobia is a tormenting, nervous complaint where a devastating panic attack strikes you out of nowhere. You convince yourself it is safer not going outside the door. At the time of the onset, I had been working as a car valet for a car hire company. I can still recall when the condition first struck: while out driving a truck, a panic attack just hit me from out of nowhere. From there on, it was a downhill route, having to leave my job and being terrified of facing people. In the company of others, I might have looked all right but, inside I seethed with fear, anxiety and panic. I always made excuses for not going to events, even when it was visiting family and friends.

My wife was my only and true friend. She was the only one who fully understood my feelings and stood beside me no matter what happened. Of course, we had growing children then but, given how young they were, they didn't understand what I was going through.

Phobias can prevent you doing the simplest things. They can interfere with all aspects of life. Night-times were really bad, when I found it hard to settle down. I found myself taking almost an hour to relax and get into sleep mode. However, after almost eight years, during which time, I studied and researched all I could on the condition, I knew I had to do something while stuck indoors. This is where the road towards journalism kicked in.

I started to write more about how I was feeling, writing everything down on paper, getting the phobias out of my system. I began writing poetry and songs and became quite good at both. I even won a literary award for one of my poems.

But that was not enough, and I began to get interested in shorthand writing. On one occasion I came across a book on shorthand and was fascinated by the way you could write two or three words with just one symbol. I couldn't put this book down and I soon became reasonably good at shorthand writing.

My daughter was studying in college by then and she managed to get me a mechanical typewriter on loan. I was amazed at the idea of me learning to type. But I was determined that I would do it the right way – no one finger typing for me! So, I began practising typing, a-s-d-f-j-k-l-… That's the way I continued until I perfected the skill. No looking at the keys as I was typing, instead, focusing on the paper I was typing from. These skills have proven more than useful in my career.

But getting over my phobias was still a block. Thankfully, however, I eventually overcame this fear and got into the wider world again. It was mainly thanks to the massive support of my wife, three children and pet dog. I was given a dog as a gift and this was a big step in getting me out and about.

Sam was a cross between a Labrador and an Alsatian. He was a very friendly dog and particularly good with children. He brought lots of love to our family and, looking back, he was very important in helping me recover. He would look at me as if to ask, in his doggie language, 'Are you taking me for a walk?'

I was responsible for taking Sam on his walkies. Each day, despite what I had been through with agoraphobia, I would go a little further, with Sam trotting along on the lead. He did not walk to heel but he took great strides in sniffing along the paths. In some ways, he was the one who was taking me for a walk.

Feeling easier, I gradually took longer walks in the park and around the area. At that time, I lived in a place called Poppintree, about a mile up the road from Ballymun. And soon, I even began taking long walks on my own – after eight years hiding in fear in my own home.

It might be overstating things to say that my dog was responsible for healing my agoraphobia but, there can be no doubt that he was instrumental in getting me out of the front door and staying out. He was a loyal pal and part of our family circle for fourteen years. Sadly, by then he became seriously ill and had to be put to sleep.

Thanks Sam for everything: you were the best friend in the world.

I have now had forty years' experience in Ballymun. Having lived in both Patrick Pearse and Joseph Plunkett Tower blocks, it was not long before I got involved in community action.

During this time, I got to know thousands of residents, officials from the council, Gardaí, other agency workers, politicians and others, many of whom were to become contacts and reliable sources for my newspaper work.

Soon after moving in, I got paid work in a Men's Network centre and a local residents' council office – a place where I began to learn about computers and printers. This led to the creation of my first newsletter. I also received some computer and internet training from a local employment service over-40s project called Workmate: something of vital importance to my later career.

While working in the men's centre, I was responsible for men's health and other issues. The centre aimed to assist with isolation and other family problems, such as separation in marriages and fathers' rights.

By then, my role mainly involved preparing the monthly newsletter for the group and communicating with other men's groups throughout the country. The writing, together with the computer training from Workmate and my own skill set, all played their part in producing a good quality newsletter.

I also began writing for newspapers locally, including the *Northside People* and *Local News*, covering stories pertaining to Ballymun. This was all a learning process, in which I was building up more and more experience, interviewing people and taking photos. Soon, I became proficient enough to start writing for the national press. My confidence grew with each story published. Then I had my first by-lined story published in *The Star* daily morning newspaper.

Receiving my first pay cheque from a national title was a tremendous wonder for me, considering that I had had very little education, never went to college or accessed formal training in journalism. But many years ago, I had been fascinated by the newspaper production I had seen on my rounds as a delivery boy. Even if I had come to journalism late, I was confident that I had the skills to run with the kind of positive-impact journalism I believed in.

At one point, I had approached DCU's Journalism faculty with the idea of studying for a master's degree in journalism. However, the head of the department (Professor John Horgan) told me that this would not be necessary. He said I already had what it took to be an instinctive, talented journalist.

Having already reported the story, "Santa Will Sleigh Them", my next big article ran in the *Irish Independent*. Within the next few months, I got more of my stories into other national newspapers. My name was now appearing in most of the national newspapers, as well as local papers.

I was now determined that I would redress the balance by reporting positive news, as Ballymun had been hard hit by negative news from sections of the media for decades. Now was time to strike back!

Having had enough paid work in national and local newspapers to qualify, I was accepted as a member of the Dublin Freelance branch of the National Union of Journalists (NUJ). Over 20 years later, I remain a member of the NUJ and it has been an honour to be accepted into a union of journalists that I admire and respect.

In both my own paper, the local and national titles, I wanted the rest of the media to recognise the difference between negative and positive reportage.

Local children greet Santa as he arrives by fire engine in Ballymun Shopping Centre, December 2003.

Christmas at Ballymun Shopping Centre, December 1999.

Christy Dignam (Aslan) with Belcare Celtic in Poppintree Park, Poppintree, Ballymun, 2002.

Young people selected for the Golf Academy with organisers and Christy O'Connor. Pictured at the Christy O'Connor Club, 2004.

Local residents waiting for Brian Kerr's arrival, 2004.

First customers in SuperValu receive free hampers, 2004.

Children enjoying a Punch & Judy show at family fun day in Ballymun Shopping Centre, 2005.

Broadcaster Joe Duffy pictured with Leane and Stacey Harcourt at major drugs meeting in Axis, Ballymun, 2003.

Rock the Blocks in the Ballymun Town Centre, 2000.

Mark O'Brien (Axis) with Elvis at Otherworld Halloween Festival, 2005.

Derek Fitzpatrick and Donnachadh Hurley in *Celebrate* at Axis, Ballymun.

Ballymun comedians Dean Scurry, Gary O'Brien, Eric Lawlor, Willie White with David McSavage (rear) in Axis Theatre, Ballymun, 2005.

Ballymun youths having action-packed fun in their new playground at Balcurris Park, 2004.

Pennies from Heaven. Children from the Holy Spirit Parish with sleeping bags for the homeless people of Dublin, 2003.

Senior citizens being treated to a party by students of Ballymun Senior Comprehensive School, 2004.

Rita's Last Stand, based on the regeneration of Ballymun, performed at Axis, 2003.

Chapter 6

The Difference between Negative and Positive News

Below is an extract taken from my personal Facebook page. In it, I try to explain, in my own way, the differences that exist between Negative News and Positive News.

Negative News Versus Positive News

Comment by Seamus Kelly, editor and administrator of Dublin Concrete News, Ballymun Concrete News 1 and Ballymun Concrete News Photo Archive.

As a veteran journalist I believe that being exposed to constant negative news and images on a near daily basis can lead to illness, emotional and psychological disorders, crime and damage to communities. Such media negativity has become the norm in our modern world and we've become almost immune to the reporting of murders, wars, devastation, corruption and evils throughout our world.

In the media, there is what might be called the copycat syndrome. Put simply, this is where some people who want to be noticed, or to display a sense of power, will tend to mimic or carry out similar hideous crimes to the ones that they see or hear in the media.

However, all is not lost. As I know from my own career, positive news has the opposite effect and can create good feelings. The copycat effect can work both ways.

Most local communities do incredible voluntary work to help others but, their positivism doesn't get the same media coverage as negative news. Granted, some members of media do file the odd smaller story now and again, that brings positivity to the attention of the general public. But primarily, it is negative news that grabs front pages and leading broadcast news.

As I have already said, I set up the Ballymun Concrete News with the objective of trying to expose good news about the local community in which I had lived for years. I believe that the stories I reported and published about Ballymun helped the local community and presented a more honest and positive image of the area. As the Ballymun Concrete News produced 20,000 free copies per month and was distributed over Dublin area, this helped dispel and change the negative image of Ballymun to a more positivistic, caring community. Currently, I voluntarily manage several positive news/ media Facebook pages. One is titled Dublin Concrete News, which I hope will have the same results, all over Dublin, as the Ballymun Concrete News.

– Seamus Kelly. Retired national press journalist. Member NUJ (National Union of Journalists). Former editor, Ballymun Concrete News. Editor, Dublin Concrete News Facebook news/media page. Editor, Ballymun Concrete News 1 Facebook news/media page. Editor of Ballymun Concrete News Photo Archive Facebook page and others.

ENDS

I'm hoping that, not only through this book but also the *Ballymun Concrete News*, national and local newspapers will realise the benefits of promoting positive news.

I believe that over the past three decades or more, in particular, we have all been exposed to some form of negative media, whether it is in the press or the broadcasting medium. From local to international news, it's mainly the same pattern of negativity all around.

In fact, I'm of the opinion that the international and local media have no concept of positive news. Over the years, they have become so used to working with negativity that they seemed to have proven the idea that negative headlines affect a person's perception of life. While I don't always agree with the promotion of major crime stories involving killings and drug wars, nor am I enthusiastic about running profiles of individual criminals or drug lords. These often get primacy of space on, not only the front pages, complete with disturbing imagery, but also within the inside pages.

I believe that positive news needs to be front-page material. I realise this is not always the intentions of the editors or newspapers. Nevertheless, they need to be aware that the effects of front page coverage can be beneficial to some criminal element.

We cannot do very much about negative international news or headlines, but we can make some changes in our own backyards (that is, our own neighbourhoods). Individuals and members of the communities can write to newspaper editors and tell them that they are fed up to the teeth reading negative stories.

Consider the impact of positive news, taking this for example, "Model Told She Would NEVER Walk Again" – a *Sunday World* centre page. This story ran on three separate occasions, always with a new angle.

Then there was the story of Sparky, a Cairn Terrier who needed wheels and nappies to get around, after he was struck on his hind quarters by a hit-and-run driver. Again, this story also ran in three different issues of the *Irish Mirror* national newspaper.

My stories got front page coverage only within my own *Ballymun Concrete News* with one exception, that of a young child who had been killed when he was struck by a lorry, while out playing with his toy aeroplane. It saddened me that such a tragic story earned the by-lined front page of *The Star* newspaper. However, as I was a local journalist, I had to cover the story albeit in a sensitive manner. Even the local priest remarked that I had done a good job reporting such a tragic story.

This was not a negative story; it was not about drugs, crime, murder or anything of a savage nature. On the contrary, this was a story which brought out the best in people when reading of such tragedy. Reader's hearts went out to the child and his broken-hearted mother. Such a story is heartfelt and it merited its place on the front page.

There are occasions when sad but heartfelt stories should appear on the front pages of our newspapers. I would rather see the kind of sad stories that bring out the best in people, highlighted by the print and broadcast media. These are far removed from the usual, crime-themed stories and pictures of savagery. Heartfelt human-interest stories tend to appear in or near to the centre pages. I know this, having reported quite a few of them myself.

My first front page story appeared in the pilot issue of the *Ballymun Concrete News* newspaper headlined, "£1.8 million Development of St Pappin's Church and Private Nursing Home for the Elderly".

"Model Told She Would Never Walk Again" – this was my report about a young model with a devastating illness, who defied the doctors' prognosis. They had told her she would be wheelchair bound for life yet, she had made a full recovery. It was exactly the sort of uplifting and feel-good story I was interested in running with. The *Ballymun Concrete News* ran this story at the same period as it ran in the *Sunday World's* centre pages.

"Ballymun Model Chosen for New York" – it was yet another *Ballymun Concrete News* front page that also ran in a national newspaper.

The first page of the official *Ballymun Concrete News* ran with, "Pool Players Snookered". This was a story about a group of boys and girls of a local pool team, who had to practice their skills in a local pub. These children were world champion pool players.

The *Ballymun Concrete News* featured reports on the positive events and stories in the Ballymun/Poppintree area and each major story was given prime space.

It was not easy running my own newspaper and trying to cover stories for the national press so, I had to prioritise. I decided that the *Ballymun Concrete News* would come first and, if I had the available time, I would also submit copy to the nationals. As over 80% of my time was taken up with chasing advertising for the *Ballymun Concrete News*, I did not have the time to report for both. Since I could not afford sales advertising representatives, I had to chase sales myself.

As I said earlier, I was completely reliant on advertising revenue to run each issue of the *Ballymun Concrete News* and could not afford to employ any staff. Running a paper on such tight resources was not an easy task. However, I had one thing and it never let me down: the very strong support of the local and business community. I was always encouraged by their words of praise for the paper and its editorial and pictorial presentation. And they were particularly enthusiastic about the emphasis on positive news. Without their support and advertising, the newspaper would have folded within a few months.

Instead, over a period of eight years, my newspaper survived, until its demise in 2006, when the prospect of a major new shopping centre collapsed, taking potential advertisement revenue with it, meaning that all chances of the newspaper's survival were dashed.

It is ironic that the largest regeneration in the history of the State could not develop a new shopping centre! This was and still is, a major setback for the local community. For decades they relied on the centre as the hub, where they shopped and interacted with other members of the community. And, from 2006 onwards, people in Ballymun have been left without a shopping centre and an independent newspaper.

But *Ballymun Concrete News'* emphasis on positive news had already made its mark and was recognised by Dublin City Library and Archives. It was viewed by them as an integral part of Ballymun's history and a journal that needed to be recorded and archived. It is currently the only newspaper to be archived on their digital website.

Although the first issue of the *Ballymun Concrete News* newsletter was issued in July 1998 and the pilot issue of the actual newspaper in 2000, it was not until 2001 that the newspaper was officially launched. It is to this event that I now turn.

Friends, supporters and guests having good time at the launch of *Ballymun Concrete News* in Axis, Ballymun, 2001.

Lena Byrne (RTÉ) with friend and local band, Columbia, at launch of the *Ballymun Concrete News*, 2001.

Sharon Kelly performs one of her songs at the launch of *Ballymun Concrete News* at Axis, 2001.

Chapter 7

Launch to Managing the Ballymun Concrete News

The official launch of the newspaper, in November 2001, took place in the Axis Arts & Community Resource Centre and was a tremendous success. However, this was a rather late launch. Up to that time, the funds were not available to have such a major celebration.

Nevertheless, although late in coming, the event was a huge success thanks to the local fund-raising support from the community, businesses, local agencies and also, the developers overseeing the regeneration programme in Ballymun. Thanks to them, I had sufficient donated funds, to provide free drinks to over 200 guests for the evening. Naturally, I was knocked for six at such an achievement.

During the celebration, a number of other journalists from local and national media, including RTÉ, were present, adding a much-appreciated journalistic atmosphere to the *Ballymun Concrete News* launch. Encouraged by the event, I became more motivated to make a success of the *Ballymun Concrete News*. But with every issue dependent on local advertising, this would not be an easy task.

Preparing for each issue was hard work that involved running all over the Ballymun area (I had no transport), searching for new advertising. I knew I could rely on my regulars although, I had to confirm that they were still on board. As said, this would take up at least 80% of my time. Unsurprisingly, I had lots of sweats not knowing if I would get enough revenue to cover the cost of the issue.

On many occasions I was just a couple of hundred short of the final figure needed for the issue. And so, I might have to ask one of my regulars to take larger space in the paper and the larger advertisement would make up the cost.

I would often debate with them about my problems gathering enough advertisements in the area, which was being regenerated and how I needed to keep the newspaper alive until the private investment arrived. But most of the time, the regulars would understand my dilemma and not let me down, sometimes even paying in advance so that I would have enough to pay suppliers – i.e. the printer and the graphic designer.

It was vital that I had the cash to pay the printer, as this would need to be paid when the papers came off the press and was my highest expense. Having said that, the printer was always very obliging and took into account the fact that I did not have much cash flow. So, he kept his costs to a minimum. I suspect it would have cost me almost double the amount elsewhere.

When times were really tough money-wise, I would have to run a fund-raising event to save the *Ballymun Concrete News* from folding. At these times, the printer was very generous in giving me three months' free printing for the newspaper. Yet, he still gave my newspaper the very best in print production.

I was always impressed with heat set as, no matter how hard you rubbed the printed paper, the ink would not rub off on your hands. This was environment-friendly printing at its best. I would often show it off to my friends, advertisers and potential customers. This aspect of the print was unique to the *Ballymun Concrete News* newspaper.

As the regeneration of Ballymun progressed, I would soon have additional advertising from building contractors. At least a quarter of a mile of a major road through Ballymun was torn up to enable building works to be carried out and a new road built. There were safety concerns around such a major road and infrastructure change. Residents and road users would need to be advised of alternative routes and any areas to avoid. The digging up of the original road also meant demolishing a roundabout, from which, five roads led into each part of the estate. I managed to convince the contractor that he should advertise the areas concerned in the *Ballymun Concrete News*. This led to a whole page each month concerning the new road, which took about two years to complete.

This additional advertising was a great asset and saw me beginning to build up a small cash flow. Each month, I was starting to see a small profit – for the first time. I was on the way or, at least, I thought so.

As chasing up adverts took up most of my time, I still had to produce and edit a newspaper with news and photos. Along with lots of positive news stories in the area, there was plenty of information about the regeneration and building work to be highlighted. Moreover, I was constantly supplied with press releases from local councillors and TDs, (elected members of Dáil Éireann parliament).

As the cash flow increased, I was at last in position to purchase the new equipment I had always needed: like a computer, printer and scanner and I could now go on the internet. Up to this point in time, I was using a fax machine for sending messages and receiving press releases and other forms of editorial. But the internet and e-mail facility was a tremendous step forward.

Like the community at large, the *Ballymun Concrete News'* hopes grew stronger with good news. This story featured on the front page of the paper, "€300m Town Shopping Centre for Ballymun".

Ballymun Concrete News now had a circulation of 20,000 copies per issue. The paper reached every home in the Ballymun area and various drop-off points throughout Dublin. I was also able to use the services of a local distributor.

Even the bank manager believed the shopping centre was coming. I guess he saw my newspaper as a good investment? Neither of us knew, at that point, that the plans would fall through, leaving me with no choice but to wind up the newspaper within three years.

The overdraft allowed for the purchase of new equipment and also helped pay suppliers and other bills, even though one or two issues had run at a loss. But making the mistake of relying on the overdraft being there, it became too easy not to worry about such expenses and overheads.

The newspaper would stay alive until the regeneration was complete and the profits started rolling in: that was the business plan. As a result, all my dreams, finances and future depended on the success of this much-needed investment in Ballymun.

As the regeneration progressed, more housing materialised, along with infrastructure, including a newly-built Ballymun Civic Centre. Advertising increased slightly during this period but not dramatically; something I found disappointing. I still had to rely on my regular advertisers and chased more local groups, looking for their support. There was a very good response from some groups and agencies. However, others who had no funding for advertising were unable to help.

The small increase in revenue helped the *Ballymun Concrete News* to survive from issue to issue, although I had to organise a fundraiser on one occasion to help keep the newspaper on the road. I had little choice in the matter, as otherwise, the paper was going to go under.

Had the printer not came to my rescue with free issues at that time, the newspaper would have been forced to close there and then. This saved me at least €5,500. (The cost of each 20,000-print run was approximately €1,700.) The saving allowed me a further three years after 2003.

In the meantime, the newspaper continued to do what it had always done: report positive news in the community and keep residents updated with the progress of the regeneration.

Stories involving the demolition proved to be of massive interest: not only to local but to the national media. The actual implosions of the tower blocks were vividly described in the *Ballymun Concrete News*, explaining in detail how the process of planting explosives in the buildings was carried out by demolition crews.

I remember on one particular occasion, in 2005, covering the demolition of the fifteen-storey Thomas MacDonagh tower block. Several hundred people, young and old, some of whom had lived there for many years, gathered to watch what promised to be a spectacular implosion. There were the usual safety precautions in place and all seemed to be going according to plan. A small delay was caused by fears that someone was still in the building. However, after a thorough search by Gardaí, the countdown began.

A young boy had been selected to push the button on the detonator, located outside the safety exclusion zone. A siren wailed and any remaining birds perched on the tower block took flight. Then it finally came!

Three... Two... One...

The explosive blast roared with all eyes focused on the fifteen-storey block, collapsing on itself to the cheers and applause of the crowd.

Applause then turned to surprise, and surprise to shock, as the crowd watched the billowing cloud of dust expanding from the exclusion zone. Some onlookers noticed that the cloud was fast heading in our direction. Suddenly people began running away from the exclusion zone, towards whatever place of safety they could reach. Among them was myself, invited guests and a Government minister, who shielded his face from the brown-grey dust as it covered us. All this was recorded in the *Ballymun Concrete News*, along with photographs of the cloud, the minister and hundreds of people running for cover.

There was yet another twist to the MacDonagh Tower implosion, but a successful one. Just three feet away from the block stood the nearby Axis centre. Both buildings were at very close proximity and so, dozens of cargo containers and rubber tyres had been piled up at the façade of the Axis centre to protect it from potential damage. And as the Thomas MacDonagh vanished forever into the huge dust cloud, there was little or no damage to the Axis building: just one broken pane of glass. In fact, the passing of the other six towers, either demolished mechanically or imploded, ended on a successful note.

All these demolitions were positive news stories. The parents of young children needed their own homes and the flats were not really suitable for young families. That is not to deny that there was a huge sense of nostalgia at the time. Some families had risen generations of children in the Ballymun flats complex and the reality of this was recorded in various *Ballymun Concrete News* stories. So, even among the cheering, there were also a few tears shed when the towers came down. As concrete became dust and machines pulled away chunks of the tower blocks, fond memories returned of living in these buildings with friends and neighbours close by.

Although working as the editor and owner of the *Ballymun Concrete News*, I recognise that covering these demolitions also had an effect on me personally. As I had lived in Ballymun for nearly forty years, and having also lived in the tower blocks, I had to hide a few tears myself on the days that Joseph Plunkett Tower and Patrick Pearse Tower were torn down. I had lived in both towers with my wife and children during our time in Ballymun. We naturally felt a strong bond, not only towards the tower building itself but, towards the other residents and friends we had as neighbours.

And of course, there was my three-bedroom flat on the tenth floor of Joseph Plunkett Tower, the last tower block to be demolished – the place where the *Ballymun Concrete News* originated. This was the finale of the old Ballymun.

Long before the Joseph Plunkett Tower's demolition however, the *Ballymun Concrete News* still had a lot of work to do reporting the news in the area. By now the image of Ballymun was fast changing, from a negative to a positive picture. The *Ballymun Concrete News* had achieved success in its mission to highlight positive news stories in Ballymun and transform outside perceptions.

Onlookers at the implosion of MacDonagh Tower, Ballymun, 2005.

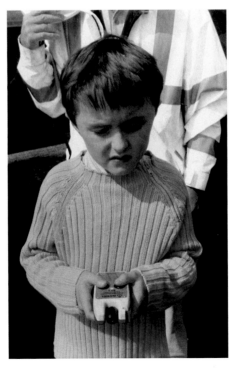

A local boy prepares to hit firing button at the implosion of the MacDonagh
Tower, Ballymun, 2005.

The MacDonagh Tower block flattened by implosion, 2005.

Minister Noel Ahern TD and crowds running for cover from dust cloud
following the implosion of the MacDonagh Tower, 2005.

Axis building untouched by the implosion of the Thomas MacDonagh tower
just feet away, 2005.

Chapter 8

The Demise of Ballymun Concrete News Newspaper

After eight years producing the *Ballymun Concrete News,* both as a newsletter and newspaper, its time was running out. I would soon be forced to shut down operations. I knew the day would finally come. With the plans for the new shopping centre scrapped and a serious lack of new business coming into in the area, the advertising revenue needed to keep my business afloat was just not coming in. I had to face reality: it was the end of the road for the *Ballymun Concrete News* and its positive news service.

Even so, I raced all over the place desperately trying to find a saviour, someone to help rescue the newspaper but with no success. My regular advertisers did all they could, including payments in advance. But this was only postponing the final and inevitable outcome. I kept closure from my mind and brought out another issue, not knowing it was to be the final issue of the newspaper.

The time finally came when I just could not secure advertising for any further issues. This was it; I had to make the decision I had been trying so hard to avoid.

However, there was a chance: a local neighbourhood council put out a tender to apply for an advertising contract. This was a group connected with the regeneration as a conduit between community and local residents on housing issues.

Putting in my application, I thought, this is my last chance. Then I waited for their response. As I was requested to submit costing for four pages of advertising over one year, I submitted the lowest costing I could afford. However, there was another newspaper, outside the area, that also sent in their quotation. As the editor of the other newspaper had more resources and a larger volume of pages and advertisers, his costs were much lower than mine. Although his newspaper was not a Ballymun-based paper, that outside publication still won the contract. I was shocked. My newspaper was not only locally based, it had been delivered to every home in Ballymun and thus was more widely accepted.

When the neighbourhood council made their decision, the final nail was decisively hammered into the coffin of my newspaper. I pulled the plug. The *Ballymun Concrete News* ceased trading in May 2006, after eight years of reporting positive news in the community. Naturally, this decision really tore me up, as I had put so much of myself into the project.

It just didn't make sense to me that a Ballymun paper, delivered free to the very people who made up the Council's target audience, was rejected in favour of an outside paper. However, the decision was made. Without the contract I could no longer continue to operate.

This also meant that I did not get an opportunity to publish the news of the closure of the paper to the community. The Ballymun community themselves were never told of the *Ballymun Concrete News'* sudden demise. It would be some time before it sunk in that the newspaper would not be arriving in their homes any more. Once they had found out, the regular advertisers and business colleagues were shocked that the newspaper was gone. They had picked up some notion from me that there were difficulties but had never perceived for, one moment, that I would actually have to let *Ballymun Concrete News* go. After all, they all knew how much I loved the publication.

As more and more people heard the news, they too reacted with disbelief. Until then, I had always managed to come through major problems and keep the newspaper alive.

I believe that it affected me the most. I found it hard to come to terms with the loss of my own creation. The *Ballymun Concrete News* had been no ordinary project. Now, not only had I lost my newspaper but, in the process, I had got into serious debt trying to keep the newspaper afloat. With bank loans, overdraft, phone bills and overdrawn debit cards to pay, I was in serious financial trouble. How was I going to repay these debts? After all, I was a sole trader and not a limited company, so I had to carry full responsibility for the financial debts of the newspaper.

For months, I was left reeling by letters of demand from the bank, threats of losing the telephone (my lifeline) but somehow, I managed to come through the worst, with a little help and advice from a local debt advice agency that helped people in serious financial difficulty. When I told them of my problems, they asked me to bring in all my bills. I did just that and first off, they told me to put the scissors to my debit card. There and then I carved the useless plastic in two.

Having examined all my bills, the agency contacted my debtors and informed them that if they wanted their money, they would have to accept nominal payments each month. As, by then, my only income was a social welfare payment, the agency sorted out what amount of money my family and I needed to live on and the remainder would go to repaying the bills.

This time was very hard for me and my family. Unsurprisingly, I suffered serious stress and was fearful that my old enemy, agoraphobia would return with a bang. Once again, going outdoors might become a panic-filled ordeal. Luckily though, I managed to keep that problem at bay.

However, sometime later, probably due to the shock of losing the newspaper and my financial debts, I suffered a heart attack. Once again, I was lucky and I got to the hospital in time.

To the immense relief of wife and family, I was not in hospital long: stents were inserted and, within few days I was allowed home. As I recovered, I reflected that I was lucky to be alive and was not going to worry about debts any more. Such a thing was not worth being ill over. I had my health and that was a much more vital thing.

Of course, living on the tenth floor of the Plunkett Tower did not help my heart condition, so my family and I moved to a bungalow in Santry, where we currently reside. I felt sadness in my heart as we departed Ballymun. This unique community had been my home for nearly forty years but, the regeneration company could not accommodate us with adequate housing, so we had to take a bungalow nearby.

Several years later, a local Fianna Fáil councillor named Paul McAuliffe phoned me to tell me that my newspaper was to be accepted into Dublin City Library archives. With my permission, the *Ballymun Concrete News* would be handed over to the Dublin City Library head archivist, to be placed within the digital library archives. This was the best news I had received from anyone since the newspaper folded. *Ballymun Concrete News* would have a whole new life. It was to be forever recorded and archived in the Dublin City Library archives and located on their website.

The *Ballymun Concrete News* lives again! This is what I thought to myself at the time. My paper would continue to inform, albeit in a city archive web page. Now, it would be available for, not only the people in Ballymun but for anyone, anywhere in the world, via the internet. And it would tell future generations a unique story of a unique community.

The actual handover of the newspaper archive CD disc to the head archivist took place at the chamber room in the Ballymun Civic Centre, the place where the local councillors held their area committee meetings. At the presentation, the head archivist thanked me for the contribution and said that the *Ballymun Concrete News* was the only newspaper archived on the website of the Dublin City Library. The moment I handed over the disc to the archivist, the newspaper went live on the web. Everyone there could see the event on the large screen in the council chamber.

This was, indeed, a day to remember, thanks to Councillor Paul McAuliffe who proposed the motion that the *Ballymun Concrete News* be accepted into the City archive, with the approval of the Dublin North West area committee.

But this was not to be the end of my work as editor of the *Ballymun Concrete News*. Before the newspaper was archived, I was invited by Professor Stephen Knowlton of Dublin City University to talk to a group of his international media students about journalism and my experiences creating a unique, positive news service.

This was an honour for me, having had no college education and yet, here I was, lecturing to students from all over the world about my journalistic career. Naturally, I did not waste such an opportunity and spoke to the students about the importance of positive news, both local and national.

This boosted my confidence and made me think, could I possibly run another newspaper on a voluntary basis, now I had reached retirement age? Not far off my seventies, I decided to use all the photographs I had taken for the *Ballymun Concrete News* and put them on a Concrete News Facebook page. I named the page Ballymun Concrete News Photo Archive.

Chapter 9

The Concrete News Has a New Life

The recognition the *Ballymun Concrete News* received through being archived by the City archives, photo exhibit and lectures vindicated its policy of concentrating on positive news only, stories that boosted self-esteem and a positive sense of self within the community.

Looking back, I believe my newspaper contributed towards and appealed to the good in people through the stories it ran. The recognition by the City also inspired me to try and extend positive news through the internet. Of course, I had no funds to start another newsletter or newspaper. Therefore, the only real option open to me was to create a Facebook page.

In fact, I began by starting three pages: Ballymun Concrete News 1 (BCN 1) and Ballymun Concrete News 2 (now discontinued), along with Dublin Concrete News (DCN). As I was too old to run all over the place chasing stories, I enlisted the help of the freelance journalist, Tom Farrell, who offered to cover and report the stories for both pages.

This was a tremendous help and, in return, I would teach him news reporting. Tom already had experience as a features writer and wrote for major national newspaper and international magazines. However, he wanted to learn more about newspaper reporting. This was to be a mutual agreement and on a voluntary basis. Within a short period, from early 2016 onwards, we had built up a number of stories and photographs.

However, the internet and Facebook cannot compare with hard copy tabloid or broadsheet newspapers you don't have to view on a screen. However, Facebook was the only resource available, free of charge, where I could continue to report news. There are, however, advantages to posting news stories online. For example, you will get comments, likes and the sharing of a story between pages. Thus, I had some idea of how favourably each story was received. Sometimes, we would get lots of likes and comments, other times not so many – something you don't get with a newspaper.

Also, if you make mistakes or want to change some editorial, you can re-edit the posts or add an update to the story. But again, this was not the *Ballymun Concrete News* newspaper of the old days. When working online, the editorial does not get the same or even similar layout as the pages of a newspaper: you have to contain the news and photos in a single post.

There is a view that the internet will eventually replace the actual hard copy newspapers. I don't think they will ever fill the void that will remain if there is no hard copy, which readers like to feel in their hands. There is something special about handling a newspaper, throwing it on the table or office desk, carrying it in your pocket on the bus, train or whatever mode of transport you use. It is something you cannot do with digital media.

Consider the alternative. First you have to go online, search for your particular paper and then scroll through the lengthy page to find your story. It is time absorbing and annoying for users to go through this routine, every time they want to view a particular item. In the newspaper you just turn over the pages and glance at what takes your interest. You can do the crosswords and perhaps enjoy the cartoons or other similar puzzles. The internet just focuses on the stories and photographs.

However, the upside is that the Facebook pages ensured that the *Concrete News* remained alive and spreading the positive news, not only all over Dublin but the digital world.

If the internet is the only way in which I can report that news, then it is worth the price. Knowing the *Concrete News* is still active, albeit via the internet, has restored my confidence in knowing I can still achieve my dream.

This book is another form of reaching out and telling the world that there is another type of news available to replace negative news. I believe positive news leads to positive living.

It's time for change throughout the media world and I believe the *Ballymun Concrete News* contributed to that different concept of positive news reporting. I realised this in the early days of the *Concrete News*, as the media showed great interest in the way in which I produced my newspaper. There was certainly interest in the work I did. I have been featured in a number of newspapers and also, in an RTÉ TV *City Folk* documentary, talking about the *Ballymun Concrete News*. I also took part in a Newstalk radio programme, where I was invited, as editor of the *Ballymun Concrete News*, to discuss current news reporting.

I agreed to be a guest on the Newstalk 106FM radio programme alongside other editors, discussing news and stories from my newspaper. Although the presenter tried to get me to comment on different areas of news, I said I was there to discuss Ballymun news only; there were other editors present who could discuss different topics. So, I stood my ground on Ballymun stories. (Ballymun was always popular with media, due to its high profile, massive high-rise housing estate. So, I usually got some decent talk time.).

The programme presenter wanted me to do a weekly spot but I was too busy running my own paper, so I agreed to a once-a-month spot. This was all down to the popularity of the *Ballymun Concrete News*. Not only did it report responsible positive news but looked as good if not better than any daily tabloid. I recognised, by this radio station's offer to have me on, that they took my newspaper seriously.

I believe that this interest would never have come about if the concept of positive news as a vehicle for positive change was not a real one.

Editor of *Ballymun Concrete News* with his wife, Kay and grandchildren pictured with *City Folk* film crew and RTÉ producer, Mary Martin.

RTÉ features *Ballymun Concrete News*. Seamus being featured for documentary outside Ballymun Civic Centre, interviewing local man.

Chapter 10

The Power of News Media

As the *Ballymun Concrete News* proved, there was a need for this type of news and it helped the local community as soon as it was made available.

Covering local good news stories is about the local people, events, groups who are proactive within the community. The work these individuals and groups do benefits their own neighbourhood. However, usually it is the bad news that grabs the media's attention.

When tragic events unfold, the media are usually on the spot within hours. On the other hand, the good news goes almost unnoticed by the media and that's where the *Ballymun Concrete News* and my national press reports came into the equation. The paper's purpose was uplift to the people involved, as they were now receiving press attention.

The power of negative news can affect particular communities. I'm not saying the bad news should not be reported. However, it's the presentation of the news which is very important. For example, I was asked on one occasion, if there was a murder in the area, how I would report the incident. I was able to reply by saying I had already covered such a story, by focusing on how rapidly the Gardaí caught the criminal, rather than opening the story with a dramatic account of the murder itself in the headline.

There seems to be a lack of sensitivity in reporting such serious crimes from the press and broadcast media. There are victims involved; communities are also affected. It is important that editors keep this in mind. Then, perhaps, there would be a more humane and sensitive approach to the reports.

I know of one particular Sunday tabloid that often runs front-page stories about criminal gangs, drug lords and the murders they commit. Not only that, in a lot of cases, there is often a biography of individual criminals on the inside pages. I've often referred to this particular tabloid as a criminal journal because the front and inside-front pages tend to be devoted to these criminal stories and presenting historical profiles of them.

Perhaps there are those who want to read this type of material but, there are other magazines that provide for that.

Then, I often read other stories carrying exposure of political corruption, fraud in the banks or financial institutions, or even the most recent exposure of the health service and the thousands of seriously ill patients left waiting, perhaps years, for their surgery or treatment in hospital. As I see it, this type of news reporting is good news, as it wakes up the health service, the government and various health officials. It also grabs the hearts of the general public and encourages empathy towards innocent people hanging on by a thread, in some cases, for urgent hospital medical attention.

In my career, I've done several human-interest stories but they could not be called negative stories, as they generate goodwill from the general public towards the plight of the people involved. Such reports do not hurt the person portrayed in the story, their friends or families and, in fact, they have a positive effect within the community. Besides empathy, sometimes offers of help are forthcoming. Poignant human-interest stories can bring out the best in the general public.

On the other hand, negative stories about murders, gang wars and serious criminality have the opposite effect. In most cases, these negative stories can generate more anger, hostility, feeling bad and uneasiness. There are also very sensitive people, for whom being exposed to excessively negative news for long periods may do psychological damage. In extreme cases, there can be the copycat syndrome, where crimes can be duplicated for reasons of attention seeking.

Ballymun had over one hundred groups all over the area, doing good work within their community. These included sports and arts groups, women's groups and activist groups. This is something that I was proud to be a part of, as both an activist and journalist.

During the course of my journalistic career in Ballymun, I had received hundreds of calls from news editors to get information or to cover some local stories in the Ballymun community. I believe that most news editors were aware, not only of the *Ballymun Concrete News* and the type of positive news I covered but also, the reliability of the contacts and sources I had built up over the years. So, in this regard, I was lucky to get so many Ballymun-themed positive stories published in national press.

At a time when the community needed plenty of outside investment, this was most important. Even if many of the promises were not kept (e.g. the technology park and the new shopping centre), it was still a major achievement to have brought out a newspaper that could raise the profile of the community in a positive and upbeat way. I have included in this book, a number of newspaper cuttings and accounts of stories that were published in the press and the *Ballymun Concrete News* newspaper (see *Chapters 15 and 16*).

The power of positive news really contributes to the profile of the area and, in this instance, Ballymun. It is important for readers to know that an area like Ballymun is just as good as any other neighbourhood in Dublin.

In the past, Ballymun had garnered a very poor and utterly undeserved image. Back then, when residents were looking for work, they complained that they could not get jobs with a Ballymun address on their CV or letter of application. Sometimes, they even had to resort to using the address of a relation who lived elsewhere in Dublin if they were realistic about getting the job.

However, when I hit back with the *Ballymun Concrete News* and my reports appeared in the national press, the image of the area began to improve. Yes, the regeneration was a distraction from normal, everyday life in Ballymun. The residents had bravely survived the onslaught of digging, demolition, building and construction works, together with excruciating levels of noise and all that goes with the tearing down of a town and its rebuilding.

It was important that there was positive news to help uplift the spirits of a people exposed to the grind and clatter of construction on what was the largest building site in Ireland. There were piles of rubble from demolished flats and from early morning onwards, lorries raced from site to site. Some of the construction work damaged underground electrical wiring and water pipes, often affecting the heating and power in the area.

While most of the talk in the various parts in Ballymun generally involved complaints about the building works, the *Ballymun Concrete News* news would provide a sense of relief, by allowing them to read of something positive. The stories and pictures in the *Ballymun Concrete News* would usually be the topic of conversation for at least a few days after publication. Usually, because the paper was local, residents would perhaps have known about the people reported in the stories and the photographs. So, the word would spread around the estate about a particular story or photograph in the *Ballymun Concrete News*, or one of my national press reports.

The newspaper filled a void, as it were. It relieved the stress of Ballymun being a constant, ongoing building site. A number of residents would often comment that Ballymun had become the largest building site in Ireland, with residents living in the middle of all this work. Keeping the feel-good factor alive is what rock-solid, positive news is all about.

Moreover, I have always believed that it is important, not only to report news that is fair, balanced, impartial and factual but, that does not set out to speculate or try to influence public opinion. From my experience in the newspaper business, news stories should be reported and nothing more. No opinion, conjecture or influence of any kind should be produced in newspaper reports. Throughout my journalistic career I have tried to stick strictly to the common-sense rules and guidelines laid down by the National Union of Journalists (see *Appendix*).

What my newspaper and reports in national newspapers have achieved is recognition that positive news is newsworthy. This has also been recognised by various academic sources.

In a report run by the *Dublin Concrete News* are comments by Secretary of the NUJ in Ireland, Seamus Dooley; Dublin City University College Head of Media Studies and former Press Ombudsman, Professor John Horgan; Chief Superintendent Karl Heller of An Garda Síochána, Harcourt Square and Dr Mark Boyle, National University of Ireland, Maynooth. All spoke highly of the newspaper.

The *Ballymun Concrete News* has proven itself to be a newspaper which has helped members of a community to recognise the amazing good news and works that exist within their own community. Although there has, over the years, been very negative media aimed at the Ballymun area and its people, it is clearer now that there are more positive stories in Ballymun than negative.

I believe that in any community, whether Ballymun or an affluent suburb, people are much the same. Hence, I don't think that the reporting of news should differ that much from area to area. Granted, during its own lifetime, Ballymun did receive more coverage in the mainstream Irish media because of its geographical make up of high-rise flats. Now that the flats have been demolished and the old Ballymun is no longer in view, there is not the same level of interest in the area.

At the same time, although the *Ballymun Concrete News* newspaper has also gone, there is still the *Ballymun Concrete News* Facebook page, which continues to report Ballymun news, with the same positive slant as before.

As former editor of the *Ballymun Concrete News* newspaper, I have not given up on covering stories in the area, just as I would have in the *Ballymun Concrete News*. Nothing as far as the *Concrete News* has changed. Perhaps the news reports are a little slower as, at 73 years, I am officially retired. And I must admit, without the assistance of a journalist colleague, I would not be able to physically cover news stories myself.

The Ballymun infrastructure has changed through the regeneration and the local residents have learned to adapt to the new environment, with more modern housing established after the demolition of the old high-rise town. But the news is much the same, as people still face challenges every day and activists and groups continue to work for their community. The Ballymun Concrete News 1 does what it can to report these activities.

Pat Carey, Róisín Shortall, Noel Ahern all victorious at the General Election of May 2002, which saw, for the first time, the short-lived introduction of computer voting.

Snow White and the Seven Dwarfs in Axis, Ballymun, 2003.

Audience enjoying *Snow White and the Seven Dwarfs* in Axis, Ballymun, 2003

Having fun in the young person's section of the Ballymun Snooker Hall, before its final closure in 2005.

Ballymun Snooker Hall closes after 21 years, 2005.

Family fun day in Ballymun Town Centre, 2001.

Bowling at family fun day in Ballymun Shopping Centre, 2001

Face painting at family fun day in Ballymun Shopping Centre, 2001.

Enjoying family fun day at Ballymun Shopping Centre, 2001.

Childcare launch at the Ballymun Partnership offices in the Ballymun Town Centre, 2004.

Miriam O'Callaghan (RTÉ) pictured with 7-month-old Sean Gaffney, Coultry, at the Childcare launch, 2004.

"Don't give up your day job!" Lord Mayor of Dublin, Dermot Lacey (Labour) pictured with Dextra, 2003.

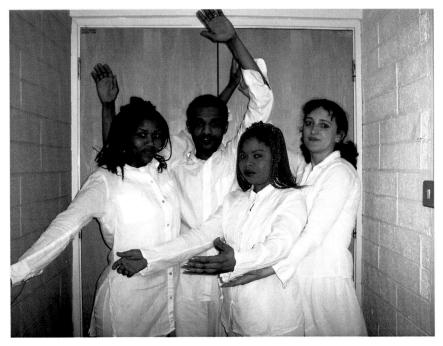

Clinela Oipela, Florence Pou Dima, Loui Osmon and Elizabeth Sich pictured before their performance of *Fall and Recover* at Axis Theatre, 2006.

Róisín Shortall TD judging Bonnie Baby Competition at Silloge Fun Day, organised by Silloge & Sandyhill Community Forum, July 2005.

Maggie Howard of Dogs Aid at pet promotion competition, 2001.

Chapter 11

The Way Forward for the Ballymun Concrete News

As the *Ballymun Concrete News* is now concerned with online media, I can't help feeling the loss of the *Ballymun Concrete News* newspaper. The newspaper was alive, it was fresh, the feel of the tabloid, colourful, pictorial newspaper in the hand. This was my dream come true.

But like all dreams, it came to an end. So, what is the future for the online newspaper, can it survive? Will it be alive? Will people accept an online version? There is a world of difference between the distribution of a printed newspaper and viewing the newspaper online on your computer or iPhone.

I've often been troubled with the idea of running a newspaper online as, to me, it takes away the personal touch. Distributing a traditional newspaper is exciting. You are bringing the news to the people in their homes and not over an internet line. This is a question being posed by all sections of the printed media at the time of writing, with sales dropping off – possibly due to the availability of fast, online news.

Yes, you can now get your latest news much more quickly and be up to the minute via the internet. The print media (including my newspaper) had to face the fact that, not only the internet but TV and radio also deliver up-to-the-minute news – something a newspaper cannot hope to compete with. Newspapers have to go through a process of page layout and preparation for the printer. Before the printing process is complete, the news headlines are already a few hours old.

However, the Ballymun Concrete News 1 Facebook page is not focused on national or international news (not for the present anyway) and local and regional newspapers can compete with the big players as online editions. There is, I believe, a gap to be filled. Local news is seldom reported on the mainstream media, unless it is through local radio.

However, there are some drawbacks to running a Facebook news page, like the Ballymun Concrete News 1 or Dublin Concrete News (DCN). Facebook is a phenomenon present throughout the word, a social media platform for anyone who wants to own or administer their own pages. It has been estimated that there are one billion Facebook pages in the world and efforts are afoot by its proprietor to expand that number. That's the competition! How can one news page like the Ballymun Concrete News 1 or Dublin Concrete News attract users to the page when there are hosts of other Facebook pages that are just as interesting or more exciting?

I have employed various techniques to try and attract more users to the page but, for the most part I found that the viewers are limited to those who are already aware of the page or have a personal interest in the Ballymun Concrete News 1 or Dublin Concrete News.

The positive side of running the Facebook page is that, unlike with newspapers, you can get immediate feedback. People can like, comment or share your news with others. The comments column gives the editor an insight as to how particular stories or photographs are being received. This is very positive and shows there is a level of interest in certain types of stories or photographs. An editor will therefore have a better idea of what kind of stories to focus on in the future.

It's a surprise to me that the Concrete News is still alive – albeit through the internet. This is not exactly the plan I had for the Concrete News but there is no way I could produce another *Concrete News* newspaper without funds or resources. When I first created the *Concrete News*, back in the 1998, I was a lot younger and in better shape health wise. Now, at the age of 73, with heart condition, on medication and other age-related problems, I can just about manage the Concrete News Facebook pages.

I do feel particularly bad that I can no longer run around, covering the stories myself. I don't drive anymore and have not been able to do so for over thirty years, due to a medical complaint. Although this was a hindrance when running the newspaper, it's even more of a problem at my stage of life. In any event, I am retired and whatever work I do has to be voluntary, as I would not like to lose my state pension.

It is difficult to know where I or the Concrete News can go from here. All I could hope for is that the Concrete News Facebook pages have as much impact as the *Ballymun Concrete News* newspaper did. What I am hoping for is that other volunteer journalists will join the Concrete News and cover stories. I would love to introduce more journalists to the positive-news house style of the Concrete News. I believe this is one way the positive Concrete News will not only survive but spread to other media, by having trained journalists in reporting positive news.

Another dream I have is that the Concrete News will achieve all it set out to do and introduce a new concept in journalism: spreading positive news. We have seen enough negativity in the media at this stage and my career experience has proven that readers react well to stories that are uplifting and make them feel good.

There's only so much left in me. I can possibly carry on for another few years at most, editing and managing several news pages. I have been in the business of journalism for over thirty years and, looking back, I have to admit, they were some of the most fulfilling parts of my career. Journalism is a very exciting profession but, more rewarding when you see some of your dreams realised. For me, the pinnacle was creating the *Concrete News* newspaper, with my vision of positive news. Well, at least I can say that I tried my best to introduce a different kind of news: news which goes some way towards creating a better balance between positive and negative news. I know well that the positive news concept is not going to replace negative news overnight. There will probably always be a constant barrage of sensational, graphic, negative-headlined news stories. I do not expect these to vanish.

Most towns and neighbourhoods would prefer it if there was more positive news reported about their areas. They don't want to be labelled as a problem area, as Ballymun has been over so many years.

While the Dublin Concrete News and Ballymun Concrete News 1 will continue to push the positive news through Facebook, it cannot hope to reach a major national market. What I am working on now, is how to attract more web users to the Concrete News pages. While there is a facility to boost posts on the Facebook page, this costs money and this is a voluntary news page. Even I don't check out free, national newspapers online: there are too many other distractions on Facebook – like getting notifications every few minutes and so many other Google searches, etc. You can find out information on almost any subject through Googling.

I honestly don't think people are going to rely only on the internet for their news. What I have found is that, if people want to read the news, they will buy a newspaper. There is definitely something to be said about reading a newspaper article as opposed to viewing a story on the internet. While reading the paper you can fold it, crease, manhandle and turn to the particular page you need to read. You don't have to keep clicking on links or enlarging print or photographs by going into viewfinder. The tactile, turning the pages of a newspaper cannot be duplicated on the internet.

There's so much hard work in trying to read a newspaper online and I say this, in spite of the fact I have my own web pages. However, there is one major advantage to getting news from the internet and that is that the news is up-to-the-minute. You get the news the moment it breaks, unlike the reports that run in the newspapers, which can only be read the following morning.

So, which is more important: reading the news next day or getting the latest online, or though broadcasting media? The drawback of TV and radio is that you must wait for the hourly or half-hourly bulletin. The internet can give immediate news. Even my simple Concrete News page can give up-to-the-minute news. The problem remains though – how to attract web users and increase your audience. So, while I am not running the pages for financial reasons, as it is a voluntary news service, to run it on a professional basis, it would need to generate a profit.

Another drawback with Facebook is that, while I want the users to comment on or like my page, they usually share the story to their own or another Facebook friend's page. This is a drawback as, if I want to identify how many people read, commented, liked or shared my story. I need to somehow keep track of all the shares and their comments too. It can become a labyrinthine effort, trying to identify who has liked who's page.

If no share facility existed, it would be a lot easier to keep track of the comments and likes. I've had a number of good stories on my pages, but, whenever some person shares the page, it is then on another person's page. On the one hand, that's a good thing, as people are sharing and possibly liking my stories. However, I cannot keep track of these comments and likes if they are shared on other pages. Yes, I can identify how many people shared the story to another page but, that's where it ends. There are so many notifications coming in from different pages that you cannot keep track of one particular share.

If I had the choice of running my own newspaper again or producing news on the internet, I would choose the newspaper. There is so much more to a newspaper than just producing news and photographs. The job takes a lot more out of you but, the end result is more than worth it. There is real pleasure in holding a tabloid-sized paper in your hands and folding it away at your own pace.

Putting together a newspaper is a very complicated process, which requires much more professionalism in graphic design, page layout, printing, in addition to the reporting and editing process. All of this is what makes producing a newspaper more challenging and exciting. And once the newspaper comes off the printing press and you hold it in your hand, gazing over the end result, you can feel a sense of pride as you take in the glorious colour and print.

The newspaper requires much more skill and attention to detail than dropping text into a text box and inserting a number of photographs, as with Facebook. Of course, with the major newspaper titles on Facebook, perhaps there is a little more work and layout required. Online, you can change typos or errors, sometimes before they are even noticed; you can even add updates to stories.

While at present I am using the internet to produce the positive news, I still hope the news will reach as many people as possible. But I have to be realistic. Facebook is merely a tool that I can use to report news and produce photos on the news pages. Once the stories and photos are up on the pages, I usually sit patiently for a while, waiting for the first comment or like to come through notifications. Sometimes, it is a quick process. On other occasions, it takes a few hours as you watch how many people your story has reached.

Sometimes also, the speed of comments and likes can depend on what time the story goes up. If a given story is loaded onto the page late at night, a lot of potential readers will already be in bed.

There are times when I post a story that strikes a chord with lots of people. It may be a story about someone who is admired and well known and suddenly, you have lots of likes and comments, as if you have won a major prize.

Perhaps the internet is the future of newspapers? Time will tell. There can be no doubt that the industry will undergo great changes in the coming years. In the meantime, I can only operate with what I have now, my Facebook pages. The important thing, for me, is getting the positive news out whatever way I can.

As I can no longer write for national press, being officially retired, my positive news service is confined to the Concrete News web pages. The stories are written in much the same style as the national press, but only positive news will run. There is still a market for this type of news reporting and it's a change from the traditional, mainly negative media coverage of our world.

Perhaps the future may see a change for the better in the media and I hope the Concrete News style will influence such change.

Chapter 12

The Ballymun Concrete News is Still Alive

Although the *Ballymun Concrete News* newspaper ceased publication in March 2006, it still exists online in a publicly accessible format. Its material is archived on Dublin City Library digital archives. The complete newspaper – all editions can be viewed via the internet.

The hard copies of the newspaper are also archived in the National Library of Ireland (NLI) and are available for public viewing at this historic library (see *Appendix*).

I think, the fact that the newspaper is archived at both these important libraries testifies that the newspaper holds a very important historic content.

See below for extracts from Dublin City Library and Archive digital web page, which also includes an introduction by the then Lord Mayor of Dublin, Cllr Andrew Montague.

Ballymun Concrete News (1998-2006)

The digital archive of Ballymun Concrete News *has been donated to Dublin City Library and Archive by Seamus Kelly and consists of 87 editions in total.*

Collectively, the papers provide a colourful record of 'good news stories' from Ballymun, from 1998 to 2006. Articles focus on topics such as the Ballymun Regeneration Project, opening of new community facilities, theatre, music, and sporting events, and the achievements of local residents in all areas of life.

Ballymun Concrete News is copyright © to Seamus Kelly.

Foreword by Councillor Andrew Montague (Lord Mayor of Dublin, 2011-2012)

I associate the Ballymun Concrete News *with the regeneration of Ballymun. The peak of the regeneration was a time of great change, and throughout that time, the* Ballymun Concrete News *told us the story of our own community. With its glossy and colourful format, the* Concrete News *always had a positive and vibrant feel.*

Seamus Kelly, the editor of the Ballymun Concrete News, *was at the heart of our community at that time. He lived in Joseph Plunkett Tower and he was a reporter who cared passionately about the community around him. Seamus made it his business to attend as many local events and meetings as possible. He always brought his trusty camera and he faithfully recorded whatever happened in both words and pictures.*

It was Seamus' passion and commitment to Ballymun that gave the Ballymun Concrete News *its heart. The paper was a constructive and positive force in the community and kept everyone up to date with all of the many changes that were going on at that time. It also gave local people a voice and place to read about their lives.*

When the paper eventually folded in 2006, it was a big loss for the community and it has never been properly replaced to this day.

I would like to pay tribute to Seamus for creating the Ballymun Concrete News. *I also want to thank all the team that put the paper together, from the first edition in 1998 to the final edition in 2006.*

ENDS

This is a massive achievement for me personally, the *Ballymun Concrete News* and the Ballymun community to receive such recognition as to be archived by Dublin City Library, on record for generations to come.

It's not just what the newspaper means to me, but the fact it was held in such high esteem by Dublin City Council's Dublin North West Area Committee. The area committee and councillors passed a motion, proposed by Councillor Paul McAuliffe (Fianna Fáil), for the newspaper to be accepted into Dublin City Library archives. The newspaper's archives were accepted by head archivist, Dr Mary Clark. This was an occasion that I will remember for years to come. What began as a simple, one-page newsletter had now become, on record, a very important part of Dublin's history.

Personally, I was amazed that someone without a formal education and mostly self-educated would receive such recognition. Never in my wildest dreams, could I have imagined such an important historic occasion for my newspaper.

The presentation of the archives took place in the Civic Chambers of the Ballymun Civic Centre, where the Dublin North West area committee held their monthly meetings.

Here I was, handing over my newspaper archive to the Dublin City Library head archivist, in the presence of the Dublin North West area committee and some fellow guests and speakers. I was also honoured to have as guest speakers, Professor Steven Knowlton, Head of Media studies, Dublin City University and John Brophy, National Union of Journalists (NUJ) speak very highly of myself and the *Ballymun Concrete News*.

The handover ceremony was introduced by the Dublin North West area committee chairperson, Councillor Dr Bill Tormey (Independent) who, on behalf of the committee, also praised my work and the achievements of *Ballymun Concrete News* over its lifetime.

As the handover of the archive disc took place, all eyes were on the huge screen in the Civic Chamber. Up there, the home page of Dublin City Library archive displayed the live image of the *Ballymun Concrete News* to a round of applause from those assembled. I just stood there, glued to the screen. This was my newspaper being spread across the internet at that very moment. I never thought that a time would come when, not only would this page be viewed in Dublin but right across the world, via the internet.

I was actually stuck for words and yet, it was my turn to take to the rostrum and say a few appropriate words of thanks. I managed to get through the nerve-racking speech and ad-libbed a bit. In all honesty, I am not a great one for preparing speeches.

After thanking my guests for attending and the committee, I posed for a few photos for the *Northside People*, a regional newspaper.

I've often wondered what it was that caused the *Ballymun Concrete News* to receive such special recognition. Was it the positive community news editorial? Was it me? Was it the recording of the regeneration process or the achievement of turning a one-page news-sheet into a newspaper? Or was it a combination of all these things?

I believe that the recognition the newspaper received was mainly to do with its uniqueness of positive news reporting.

There was also praise from other editors, politicians, academics, trade unionists, community groups and others. They recognised the amount of hard work and effort I put into producing the *Ballymun Concrete News*. They have, perhaps, seen the success the newspaper was having, not only in the local community but also, that it was becoming a talking point among other sections of the media and within the political world.

As I have previously recounted, my newspaper and I featured in a short European documentary filmed by RTÉ called *City Folk*, which aired on both RTÉ 1 and RTÉ 2 television channels. So, the City Library archive, although very special to me, was not an isolated case of recognition for the newspaper. If anything, the archive was the icing on the cake, real recognition from a highly-regarded, public City archive.

In the next chapter, I will be talking about another Facebook page I manage called Ballymun Concrete News Photo Archive. This is my own photographic archive of all the photographs published in the *Ballymun Concrete News* during its lifetime. This is, in fact, another part of the *Concrete News* that also received great recognition and led to a *Concrete People* photographic exhibition (see *Chapter 13*).

I had created a newspaper from nothing and guided it from its infancy as a one-page news-sheet to a newspaper, only to witness it cease publication. But, eight years later, it still lives today. For me this is the real achievement.

In 2006, when I lost the newspaper, I thought that it was the end and it almost broke my heart. On that point, the stress during that awful time probably led to my heart attack. But today, in 2017, it still exists, not only in the City Library and Archive but also, in the National Library of Ireland, on Facebook pages, the *Concrete People* exhibition – and now this book.

I believe positive news never dies. Negative news has a short lifespan. Do we remember the good in people in our lives or the bad? Don't we all like to recall good memories and not the hurtful, negative ones? I think it's the same with positive news and the kind of rock-solid story I championed will always be remembered, even if only in someone's thoughts.

I hope the *Ballymun Concrete News* lives on in fond memories of the many thousands (if not more) who read the newspaper. I consider myself lucky knowing that millions of people all over the world could, right now have access to my newspaper online via the City Library and my Facebook pages.

Perhaps the positive news has travelled even wider than I imagined? I may never, in my lifetime, get feedback from other parts of the world, but I know, at least, the facility is there. What's even more important is that the news and the positive editorial the paper carries worldwide, emphasising positive news, will reach a wider audience through the power of the internet.

Chapter 13

Ballymun Concrete News Photo Archive

Over the years, one special feature of the *Ballymun Concrete News* has been the photographs. More than 2,000 photos were captured for the newspaper, all taken with a humble 35mm film camera. I did not want these photographs and their negatives to continue lying in an old suitcase on top of my bedroom wardrobe. It was then that I decided to create a Facebook page, titled 'Ballymun Concrete News Photo Archive', with the objective of archiving these valuable and historic photographs.

Initially, the archive was for Ballymun people but then, the page took off and I realised that there was a world of Facebook users out there, who may also want to view the archive and experience life in Ballymun at various different times and eras.

The positive response came quickly. I was amazed at the initial reaction when I posted the first dozen or so photos. People were commenting to each other about who was in such and such photo and remembering the events surrounding the pictures. In addition to the thousands of comments, there were the usual likes and masses of sharing of the photos with friends, family and other Facebook friends.

Posting the photographs online, I would provide the reader with a short caption to accompany each one, detailing whoever was in the picture (if known), along with the year the event took place and a link to the archived newspaper at Dublin City Library digital archives. So, if users wished, not only could they see the photographs, but they could also use the link to the newspaper to view the story surrounding the images. This created a lot more hard work for me. Nevertheless, I wanted to give as much detail to the pictures as I could. My efforts would lead to some positive and surprising results in the near future.

The work involved scanning thousands of negatives on a tiny scanner (borrowed from a friend), which took me several weeks. I had to scan and name all the images. In addition to this, I would also go to the archives of the newspaper to identify the story and caption that matched each of the negatives. This was very time consuming, but I rushed through the scanning and labelling process. I wanted to get them up as soon as possible on the photo archive page. All the user then had to do was click on the highlighted text in the photo, which would automatically bring them to the page or the actual issue of the newspaper.

There was huge, positive reaction from viewers to the photos, as most people had fond memories associated with them and this would be reflected in the comments that the photos generated. And so, I felt encouraged in my efforts to upload more photos over the years and, eventually, the online archive reached over 1,400 photos and captions connected with events.

In addition to the Ballymun Concrete News Photo Archive, I was also managing both the Dublin Concrete News, Ballymun Concrete News 1 and Ballymun Concrete News 2, which are news/media Facebook pages. The arrival of these pages reinforced the notion that the *Ballymun Concrete News* really is alive and kicking again, albeit on Facebook. If the newspaper did not exist in its old format, something to be held in people's hands, I could at least still bring both news and photos to the internet.

One day, I got a nice surprise when I received a message to say there was a video of some of the photo archived pictures up on You Tube. I checked this out and there it was, true as life. Someone had put together a collection of photos from the page with background music. They had made a video of it and uploaded it to YouTube. I later found out that a staff member of the local Ballymun Partnership had put the whole thing together and uploaded it. Of course, I was thrilled as it was something I never thought to do myself. Moreover, I did not have the technical skills to produce such a video.

Using the video, I approached the local Axis Arts & Community Resource Centre manager and asked if he could use the video in the Axis art gallery. We discussed various ways in which the video could be used. He decided on an exhibition of photos from the Ballymun Concrete News Photo Archive. This was yet another achievement for the *Concrete News*.

After several meetings with the co-ordinator of the exhibition, I decided on the title, *Concrete People*. I chose this name as it represented the people of Ballymun as being a strong, close-knit community who had, over the years, suffered from being portrayed in a very negative light by various sections of the media. Yet now, there was a visual exhibition that presented an opportunity to show Ballymun in its true, positive light and with coloured photographs providing a unique view of the iconic estate.

As funding was made available to the exhibition, it never cost me one cent. In that sense, I was lucky because, in most gallery and photo exhibitions, artists usually pay their own expenses for the overheads of their exhibits, something I could never afford living on a state pension.

When we selected what photos would be displayed in the Axis, I had to choose from a collection of almost 2,000 pictures. Selecting the right ones was often a very painful decision, as I felt that all the photographs had their own value. Eventually the Axis co-ordinator chose a number of photos and I also picked out some of my own favourites. Together, we whittled the number down to 18 photos, which were chosen to go on the walls of the first-floor gallery. I must admit that it turned out to be a wise choice of photographs, representing a snapshot of Ballymun, its people and historic events as seen through the eyes of the *Ballymun Concrete News*.

There then came the question of how these photos would be displayed on the walls. Was it to be picture frames or foam boards? I was not happy with pictures in glass frames, as they tend to reflect light from overhead and to the side. So, I was pleased with the foam boards that were chosen.

The publicity surrounding the *Concrete People* exhibition was really good, with national media highlighting the event in advance of the exhibit. The *Herald* newspaper ran an article about the event and the several photographs to be exhibited. Local radio stations also posted photos on their internet pages and the local newspapers publicised news of the exhibition.

I was delighted by this level of interest. At the launch of the exhibit, when it came to my turn to speak about the *Concrete People*, as I stood at the microphone, I was overcome with emotion and had to cut my speech short. Seeing so many local people, journalist colleagues, and friends who came to see the work, I found it very hard to talk about it. However, no one seemed to notice except me.

Since the *Concrete People* exhibit was a complete success, I was also approached by a number of people wishing to buy pictures. Up to the night of the exhibit I had not even considered selling any of them, so this came as a surprise. I declined to sell any photos on the night and they remain in my home to this day. However, I am talking with Axis to see if there can be a permanent home found, where the photos can be publicly displayed for all to see.

Following the exhibit, I was contacted by the *Inquirer* who sent people to take photographs and interview me for their publication. There was also excellent coverage of the launch in the *Northside People* and the *Local News*, who were both very supportive.

Soon after, I was contacted by a Dr Mark Boyle, Head of Geography at National University of Ireland, Maynooth, requesting that I give a talk to fifty of his students and also a tour of the exhibit. I was gobsmacked to receive a request like this from such a senior lecturer at a national university.

When the coach arrived with the students, I felt nervous and rather apprehensive. I had never addressed so many people before, let alone university students. However, I need not have worried, as they made it easy for me, being very attentive to my every word. I spoke, at length, about the *Ballymun Concrete News* and the regeneration of Ballymun, since they were Geography students, studying urban development and I had some knowledge of the subject. The students had been accompanied by lecturer and tutor, Cian O'Callaghan and he proved to be a great asset in assisting me through the talk.

Perhaps it is the newspaper's ethos of Positive News, the photographs, and the uniqueness of its editorial, layout and design? Whatever the reason, the recognition is there, as shown throughout this book in other chapters.

News is the same everywhere; it is really just a question of the style and content of news reporting.

The Ballymun Concrete News Photo Archive just about sums up the story of Ballymun, as each photograph tells its own story. They say every picture paints a thousand words. Well, how about 1,400 pictures over 86 editions of a newspaper: that paints a lot of words!

This book merely recounts the story behind the *Ballymun Concrete News* newspaper, Ballymun Concrete News 1 (BCN 1), Dublin Concrete News (DCN) and the Ballymun Concrete News Photo Archive Facebook pages.

The *Ballymun Concrete News* has been the one major success of my professional life, and the photo and library archives will be a visual reminder for the present and future. But the positive news editorial, which I never strayed from throughout the newspaper's 86 editions, is the one thing that I hope I will leave to the media world.

I sincerely hope that more and more people will view, download, comment, like and share some of the photos for posterity from the Ballymun Concrete News Photo Archive.

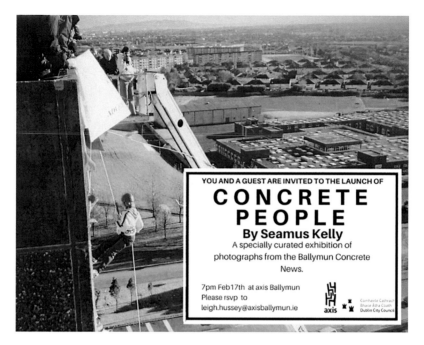

YOU AND A GUEST ARE INVITED TO THE LAUNCH OF

CONCRETE
PEOPLE
By Seamus Kelly

A specially curated exhibition of
photographs from the Ballymun Concrete
News.

7pm Feb17th at axis Ballymun
Please rsvp to
leigh.hussey@axisballymun.ie

Concrete People , a specially curated exhibition of photographs from *Ballymun Concrete News* was hosted by Axis, Ballymun.

Seamus Kelly
Concrete People

Seamus Kelly pictured at his photo exhibition, *Concrete People*, in Axis, Ballymun. Photo by Mark O'Brien (Axis).

Chapter 14

Why Did I Not Take the Newspaper outside Ballymun?

There were a number of business people who, over the years, suggested that I should take the newspaper outside the Ballymun catchment area and make more money through advertising from other areas. I declined to take the newspaper to other areas because the paper was created, in the first instance, for Ballymun, as the community needed a lifeline of positive news to reverse the negative representation from sections of the media. For over two decades the area had been portrayed by national media as a drug-ridden, crime-filled area. Nothing could have been further from the truth, as the *Concrete News* showed over its lifetime.

Sure, I could have made more money from advertising outside Ballymun, but that would have meant covering news from other areas. It also would have meant taking the name Ballymun from the title, which I was not prepared to do. My heart was with and in Ballymun, and the *Ballymun Concrete News* was created to serve the community with positive news. It was the mission statement of the *Ballymun Concrete News* to produce positive news only, in the Ballymun area and to highlight all the good news and events that made the area special.

I knew, from experience, that anyone not living in Ballymun would not have an understanding of just how much Trojan, voluntary work and heart-warming events occurred round the clock in this close-knit community. Yes, Ballymun really was a strong community and a sharing community, who watched out for each other. There was a colossal mountain consisting of thousands of positive, human-interest stories just waiting to be told and the *Ballymun Concrete News* was there to play its part in covering them.

Another important reason for not taking the newspaper to other areas is that I had lived there since 1974 and had built up a good knowledge, both of the area and the community. I had been involved in community voluntary work throughout the area for nearly forty years so, I had plenty of contacts and knowledge of how the local community worked. This proved to be invaluable, as I have covered hundreds, if not thousands of Ballymun stories.

More importantly, most of the locals knew and trusted me, both as a Ballymunner and a journalist. They knew I loved and cared about Ballymun and had proved myself through my voluntary community work. I was involved in men's groups, a community coalition, teaching children chess and, playing guitar for children's and adults' Sunday Masses in local churches. I was also a member of the Estate Forums and Housing Task Force and had a good knowledge of estate management and the regeneration project.

In addition to these and many other works, I represented a number of tenants on the estate, dealing with the council on their behalf in matters such as housing and maintenance issues. So, I had built up a bond within the community and also, with the major community leaders and activists.

It was important that, not only did I cover and report the local news but that it was sourced through the most reliable contacts, which I had built up through my community involvement. Had I taken the newspaper outside the Ballymun area, I would have been all at sea, not knowing or having any real contacts in those areas. So, I can give more reasons for *Concrete News* staying in Ballymun than I can for moving to another area. Ballymun was my home and I knew it as much as I knew myself.

Over the years, I have had people from all walks of life come to me, looking for information about Ballymun. When I speak to these people, seemingly I was their first port of call. The editor of the *Ballymun Concrete News* was seemingly the person who could answer all their queries. While it's a compliment knowing I was the first person to contact for information concerning events and community life in Ballymun, sometimes it was a little too much to deal with.

Even now, eleven years after my newspaper folded, I only just received a call from a reporter with a major Sunday newspaper, looking for information about how to find someone who lived in Ballymun. I told him I was long retired and out of touch with my old sources and contacts. There was a time, running the *Concrete News*, when I would have been able to find the information he wanted. Nevertheless, getting the call flattered me somewhat.

I was also glad to receive a call from an old colleague who worked for a newspaper I had written for in the past. We had a good chat about journalism in general and how Ballymun has changed since the major regeneration. Since the building of the new town, thousands of residents have moved, either to other areas or new homes in Ballymun.

I am proud that I decided to keep the *Ballymun Concrete News* in the Ballymun area and believe I have achieved what I set out to do.

I honestly don't think the *Ballymun Concrete News* would have worked in other areas. As I didn't know them well, it would have been extremely hard to identify the advertising market, working alone and not having any contacts or sources in the district. In fact, the paper probably would have folded after a few months, due to lack of advertising and really good, positive news.

In addition to this, I think each area would prefer to have its own identity and its own publication. While there are regional newspapers, most places still do not have their own local publication, like Ballymun. Other communities need to produce a similar newspaper of their own, as they have their own individual stories to tell, just like we did. For that reason alone, I am honoured to have created the *Ballymun Concrete News* just for one community and do not regret not going outside the area.

What I have tried to do, in addition to producing positive news in the Ballymun area, is to introduce a new concept in news reporting by publishing positive and well-presented, factual, impartial and balanced news. You could call it a pilot project, testing the market for positive news in the modern media. Would this have worked in other areas is another question. I can only speak for Ballymun but, I would suspect that other communities who suffered bad press would also find positive news refreshing and a novel experience.

My newspaper has proved, beyond doubt, that there is a huge amount of good news in an area labelled disadvantaged; surely this is a lesson which can be built on by other national media? While I recognise there is a need for national and regional newspapers, there is an even bigger need (as shown in Ballymun) for local newspapers, producing positive news. There is no doubt in my mind that keeping the newspaper focussed on Ballymun has been the right choice; each area should publish its own community news.

I often wonder, had Ballymun been a more affluent area, would a *Ballymun Concrete News* have been more successful? I doubt it, as the need is not as great as in a disadvantaged area. Of course, I am not saying that affluent areas don't need their own positive, community newspaper. They do but, in some communities, the need is greater than in others.

These are people who were treated poorly by governments and councils over the decades and yet, the community as a whole managed to fight back, by organising themselves into tenants' associations, coalitions and community groups. It was these organisations which, over a period of time, showed they had true grit and, by constant action, pushed the council and government to introduce a massive €2.5b regeneration scheme.

In summing up, I will say that the best decision I made was keeping the *Ballymun Concrete News* a local Ballymun newspaper, although it folded due to the promised shopping centre not being delivered. Had the shopping centre been built, there is no doubt that the newspaper would not only have survived but would have expanded. However, I am still happy that I decided to keep the newspaper alive in Ballymun and now that the newspaper has gone out of print, I can honestly say that I gave it my best shot.

Left to Right: Michelle Delaney, Vicky Killeen, Patricia Brennan, Anita Nolan
hold picture of Columbia in *Ballymun Concrete News* in Axis, 2001.

Children enjoying their new playground at Éamonn Ceannt and Connolly Towers.
"It's Brilliant," said the boys and girls. "We've never had a better time." 2002.

Roundabout Theatre players at the vacant flat in Ballymun, where they are performing *Tumbledowntown*, 2005.

President Mary McAleese meets traveller children at St Maragarets, Ballymun, 2005.

President Mary McAleese with Axis Director, Ray Yeates, arriving to launch Axis programme for 2005.

On your bike. Local boys and girls outside Ballymun Civic Centre with the recycled bicycle, 2005.

Showing off their gold and bronze trophies are the boys and girls who took part in the under-8s athletics finals in Dublin and Mosney, Co. Meath, with coach Mary O'Rourke at Balcurris Park, Ballymun, 2002.

Balcurris Balbutcher Community Active (BBCA) girls race at the Community Games in Balcurris Park, Ballymun.

Garda Inspector in charge of Ballymun, Karl Heller and Garda Sergeant Bernard Young at the Otherworld celebrations in Ballymun, 2005.

Garda Operation Assist in Ballymun. Local children and mothers pictured with Garda horses, Lir and Cara and mounted Gardaí, 2001.

Linx members about to have lunch. Brendan Bent is seated left. 2004.

Ballymun Senior and Junior teams and coaches of the Irish Pool Federation at Axis, trying to raise funds for team, 2003.

The first ever café bar pub quiz in Axis, Ballymun in aid of the Drop In Well Centre

Participants in the pub quiz, representing the Job Centre and the Drop In Well Centre.

Men's Centre, Ballymun taking part in café bar pub quiz.

Chapter 15

Ballymun Concrete News Stories

I recall, with fond memories, the hundreds of stories and photographs both published and unpublished in the *Ballymun Concrete News*, since its creation in 1997. The stories for me were special, in that they were all positive and focused on the Ballymun community and the area, which also included the regeneration.

Among the special stories I can recall is a visit by the President of Ireland, Mary McAleese, to a group of people suffering mental health issues, when she dropped into their centre for a cup of tea and a chat. This was in March 2004.

The group, called ACORN, consists of people who are mental health sufferers (as they called themselves) and want to empower each other and live lives to the full. They met in an old basement flat at the eight-storey block of flats in Balbutcher Lane, Ballymun. The basement was not exactly a palace and some of the furniture was old, including the armchair President McAleese sat on, drinking her tea whilst chatting with the group.

However, the President spent almost an hour in conversation with the group, which included myself, as I was there to record the event for the *Ballymun Concrete News*. This indeed was a special visit to a special group of people and, to have the President visit them in their own environment was indeed a tribute to the group and the area.

"Rock the Blocks" was yet another story that featured in *Ballymun Concrete News* in August 2000.

Rock the Blocks was both an annual and biannual musical event, which took place in the Ballymun Town Centre. Ballymun bands from all over the area took part in a rock extravaganza – to the thrill of local residents gathered in the shopping centre car park. The music event would include Rock, Ballad, Irish Folk and Jazz. The audience cheered and rocked with the beat of the music.

The *Ballymun Concrete News* ran a whole page dedicated to the event, which helped show Ballymun in a positive light, with young people providing spectacular entertainment.

In the November/December 2000 issue of *Ballymun Concrete News*, we featured the Irish soccer international, Tony Cascarino, paying a visit to the local Senior Ballymun Comprehensive School, to the thrill of the youngsters. As part of their transition year, the students received the surprise when the soccer star walked into the school library. This was a memorable day for the school, students and the *Ballymun Concrete News*.

The newspaper reported a group of brave students who took on a towering leap to raise money for a cancer research charity, by abseiling down a fifteen-storey tower block in Ballymun. The young Leaving Certificate students from Ballymun Senior Comprehensive School were hoping to raise over €1,000. This was another example of Ballymun's young people doing their bit for a good cause.

In January 2002, "Historic Discovery is Unearthed at St Pappin's" was an exclusive, special, front-page report in the *Ballymun Concrete News*.

Human skeletal remains were discovered in St Pappin's Church grounds, Ballymun, where Woodgreen Builders were beginning a €2.54m project to build a private nursing home for the elderly and also renovate the church.

Woodgreen were in the process of building a nursing home for the elderly at the rear of the 156-year-old St Pappin's Church, which is a listed building. During an archaeological dig, which was undertaken as a part of the works, the 200-year-old human remains were discovered in a tomb on the church grounds. The remains were believed to be those of James Kelly, a coachman who was employed by Lord Domville of Santry, around 1800.

Again, this was good news for Ballymun: an exciting discovery and a new nursing home for the elderly to be built next to the church.

In June 2002, we ran the story, "Children's Opera Comes to Axis Ballymun Theatre", in which we reported and reviewed the opera, *Quest*. This was performed by the National Chamber Choir, involving one hundred children hailing all the way from Cork to Dublin.

This was very good news for Ballymun – that the arts and opera were performing in the area. It certainly showcased a positive community and was portrayed in colourful photography in the *Ballymun Concrete News*.

The Axis centre also featured the Traveller Women Artistic Mural, created by the St Margaret Traveller Women group. I reported it in the newspaper and it was good news because only very seldom did the women receive recognition for their work.

In June/July 2005, yet again, another *Ballymun Concrete News* story on Ballymun Travellers. Headline, "President Presents Health Awards to Ballymun Travellers".

As reported in the newspaper, President McAleese presented a group of Traveller Women at St Margaret's Community Centre, Ballymun with certificates, having completed a course in primary health care. This was a tremendous achievement for them and especially having the President of Ireland, Mary McAleese, present the awards.

One remarkable story covered in *Ballymun Concrete News*, in April 2001, was the making of *Bloody Sunday*, a film shot in Ballymun flats complex, based on the tragic events of 1972 at the Rossville Flats in the Bogside of Derry, Northern Ireland, in which 13 civilians were shot dead by British soldiers.

During the making of the film, thousands of people lined the streets of Ballymun as film extras. The low budget, £4m film, co-produced by Jim Sheridan's company, Hell's Kitchen, in association with Portman Film, was being shot around Derry, Northern Ireland and different locations around Dublin, including Coultry Road in Ballymun.

The film re-enacts the events of *Bloody Sunday*. Along with my tiny, trusted camera, Dictaphone and notebook, I spent the complete day covering the story, side by side with thousands of film extras and actors who were acting out the scenes for the cameras of that tragic day.

It was good news for Ballymun to be chosen as a location for such a major film, soon to be shown in major cinemas across Ireland and throughout the world. Ballymun people, alongside thousands of other Dublin people were being recorded on film, portraying a sad part of Irish history, never to be forgotten. Hundreds of local people were employed as extras in the making of the film.

Among the cast included leading actor, James Nesbitt as civil rights activist and member of the Northern Ireland parliament at Stormont, Ivan Cooper. Playing the role of a Catholic priest was Don Mullan, author of *Eyewitness to Bloody Sunday* and co-producer of this film.

I spent the day covering and taking photographs of the historic event for my own newspaper, the *Ballymun Concrete News*.

These are just a sample of the hundreds of positive stories to be publicised in *Ballymun Concrete News* over the years since its creation. There are many more happy, positive and memorable stories in the newspaper and photographs, which can be viewed at Dublin City Library online digital archives. Alternatively, the hard copies can be viewed, by appointment, at the National Library of Ireland (see *Appendix*).

While all the stories reported in the *Ballymun Concrete News* have been positive and good for the community, there have been some stories about the regeneration of Ballymun that did not have happy endings.

Next is an example of how two major potential investors, who were to invest in Ballymun, create thousands of jobs and would be good for my newspaper business, failed to get projects off the ground.

February 2001: A special report in the *Ballymun Concrete News* tells of the Ballymun Regeneration Ltd (BRL) plans to bring jobs to Ballymun through the massive €2.5b regeneration of the area. Although the plans were very ambitious, it raised big hopes for the area that major investment would bring massive employment to the area (which turned out to be a major disappointment to Ballymun residents).

The report also detailed the plans to bring in over 1,000 jobs with the development of a Business and Technological Park. In the exclusive report, managing director of BRL stated that "at least 1,200 Ballymun residents will get new jobs."

Unfortunately, the Business Park failed to materialise over the lifetime of the regeneration.

August 2001: "Treasury Holdings to Develop Shopping Centre" ran as front-page story on *Ballymun Concrete News*.

The report stated that Treasury Holdings purchased the shopping centre from John Sisk, for €6m and, in partnership with Havenview Ltd, Treasury planned to redevelop the old shopping centre as part of the regeneration. This was good news for local residents, as the area needed a new shopping centre. The old one was becoming almost derelict and more retailers were pulling out of the centre.

John Bruder, Director of Property at Treasury Holdings said, "We are making good progress in our active negotiations with Dublin Corporation and we are confident that a partnership approach to the scheme should ensure a speedy delivery of this project, which is a cornerstone of the overall regeneration programme."

This was the initial plan, which was hoped would address the urgent need for a vibrant new shopping centre. However, it was not until August 2003 that the shopping centre plan was announced in *Ballymun Concrete News*: a €300m shopping and leisure centre complex, covering in excess of one million square feet, planned for the area over five years to replace the old centre.

According to Treasury, the planning application had been made and they aimed to begin work on the new shopping centre in 2004. The plans were also advertised by Treasury Holdings in the *Ballymun Concrete News*. More amazing news, especially for residents and *Ballymun Concrete News*. This meant I could now make plans to grow my newspaper, with the incoming retail to be located in the new shopping centre.

In May 2005, the news was finally announced at a Dublin City Council Dublin North West Area Committee meeting by Treasury Holdings' consultant, Murray Adair, that the Phase 1A of the €300m shopping centre was to begin within a few weeks (in June). A number of units were to be built on Silloge Road near the Supervalu supermarket on the Main Street. It was also stated, by Murray Adair in the *Ballymun Concrete News*, that 1,000 jobs were expected to be created in the construction process.

John Sisk was contracted to carry out the building of the new centre. However, a major dispute later developed between Treasury Holdings and Dublin City Council and it was reported in the *Irish Examiner* (see *Appendix*) that the disagreement was over the price of the land.

Plans for Phase 1A of the shopping centre were thus dropped and this left my business in a mess. This was a bitter pill to swallow, as my business was already struggling to survive. The current shopping centre tenants were dwindling faster and faster and the advertising was drying up for the newspaper.

Eventually, having exhausted all avenues to try and save my newspaper, I decided there was no choice but to close my business in March of 2006. No new shopping centre and no *Ballymun Concrete News*!

While all these plans for the shopping centre were good news, and reported in the *Ballymun Concrete News*, I felt let down that neither Treasury, BRL nor Dublin City Council advised or warned me the plug was to be pulled on the centre. With the disaster of losing both the Business and Technological Park and the newly planned shopping centre, this was the final nail in the coffin for any major investment, which would have delivered over 2,000 jobs to Ballymun and turned my newspaper into a financial success. A report in the *Irish Examiner* ("Ballymun; From High Hopes to Broken Dreams", 3 August 2015) by Seamus Kelly (myself) and Tom Farrell, looks at the matter in more detail. It can also be viewed online (see *Appendix*).

Having said all that, there are aspects of the regeneration which have been good for the area. However, they did not produce the thousands of jobs or investment the area needed. These can also be viewed in the archives of the *Ballymun Concrete News*.

Today Ballymun has no *Ballymun Concrete News* and we are left with a shadow of a once vibrant shopping centre, which is now a ghost town.

Film extras for *Bloody Sunday* in Ballymun Shopping Centre, 2001.

Crowd scene for *Bloody Sunday*, on location at Shangan Road, Ballymun, 2001.

Cameraman filming tear gas scene for *Bloody Sunday*, 2001.

Dramatic episode of priest rushing to aid injured man in scene from
Bloody Sunday, filmed in Ballymun, 2001.

Leading actor, James Nesbitt at the filming of *Bloody Sunday* in Ballymun, 2001.

Don Mullan, author of the eyewitness *Bloody Sunday* book, plays the part of a Catholic priest in *Bloody Sunday*, filmed in Ballymun, 2001.

Chapter 16

More Ballymun Concrete News Stories

There are other stories, which the *Ballymun Concrete News* covered and reported on in the early newsletters, from 1998 to 1999. Below is a list of the stories which, like those in the newspaper, are positive although, there are no photographs, as I had no equipment at the time to scan or produce them.

2 September 1998

Headline: Army Gives Ballymun Residents a Lift

An emergency Irish Army operation went into action in Ballymun, to rescue local residents stuck without lifts in the high-rise housing estate as a lift strike worsens.

As strikers withdrew their emergency service in the area, Dublin Corporation's Regional Office in the shopping centre became the army's centre of operation

'Aid to The Civic Community'.

Soldiers from the Fifth infantry battalion, McKee Barracks, under the command of Commandant Michael Kelly and the Assistant City Manager, Mr Brendan Kenny, put their plans into action to help the residents get back into their homes.

This was a tremendously positive story, with the Irish Army troops springing into action, helping families with their children and shopping up the fifteen and eight-storey stairwells, the lifts being out of action.

A further newsletter, on 12 September (ten days later), reported that both the army and management of the lift company began fixing those lifts needing repair, while the strike by the lift workers continued.

7 December 1998 Newsletter

Headline: Dog to Get Wheels for Christmas

(From my report in the Ballymun Concrete News and the Irish Mirror, Monday, 7 December)

A young terrier dog that can't wag his tail or walk with his back paws, is expected to get a special cart on wheels this Christmas, so he can go out for walks. Three-year-old Sparky, a Cairn terrier, is paralysed due to a spinal injury after being knocked down by a motorist on Balcurris Road in Ballymun.

But, with the love and care of Dog's Aid voluntary worker, Maggie Howard, an animal lover and carer in the area, the brave canine is now dragging himself around her home quite happily.

Two weeks later, on 28 December, *Ballymun Concrete News* followed up with the headline, "Brave Dog, Sparky, Gets His New Wheels for Christmas".

Just seven days before Christmas, the *Ballymun Concrete News* and the *Irish Mirror* reported that Sparky, the terrier, received his parcel from America, containing a special cart on wheels, to help him go walkies. This was a great human-interest, positive-news story about the rescue of a badly injured dog and, with the love and care of the Dogs Aid voluntary worker, Maggie Howard, the animal made a full recovery.

My story on this dog was reported in three different editions of the *Irish Mirror*, each with a different angle to the story, which was very popular with the readers. In one particular edition, the *Irish Mirror* used the Sparky photo on their front-page banner. This was a huge compliment to a powerful positive, human-interest story emanating from Ballymun.

In issue dated 21 January, the *Ballymun Concrete News* reported the story of two local women raising funds for an animal centre, headlined, "£250,000 Raised for Ballymun Animal Centre".

The story as reported at the time:

Over £250,000 in funding has been raised, by two women, for the setting up of a unique, all animal centre in Ballymun. The centre, which is expected to be the first of its kind in Ireland, is proposed to cater for horses and all animals in need of shelter, care and veterinary treatment.

Under the umbrella of BACA (Ballymun Animal Caring Association), both Dog's Aid and the Ballymun Horse Owners Associations aim is the protection and welfare of all animals.

The two women were Victoria McElligott of BACA and Maggie Howard of Dogs Aid (who also cared for Sparky, the paralysed terrier dog). At the time, according to BACA, some of the proposals for the animal centre were to include a veterinary hospital, stables for horses, kennels for dogs and special areas for other animals. Yet another positive story about Ballymun, which was also reported in my newsletter and in the *Sunday People*.

Another positive story reported in the *Ballymun Concrete News* was headlined, "Artists Do Ballymun Proud at Art Exhibition". This was a story about 200 local artists displaying their works at the Dublin Corporations Civic Offices.

The storyline ran something like this:

Old breadboards, coloured with artistic paintings, were the subject of the day for one Ballymun artist at the Mun Art exhibition in Dublin Corporation Civic Offices this week. The creative paintings, depicting human misery through poverty and unemployment and other works, including Ballymun buildings, were painted on old breadboards by Mr Tom Shannon, the well-known Ballymun artist supreme.

Mr Shannon [now deceased], is just one of the many artists who took part in the colourful art exhibition in the Atrium room at the civic building. With 17 exhibits of over 200 artistic works from The Association of Ballymun Artists (ABA), the artists took great pride in displaying their talents, in all forms of art, at the exhibition. The exhibition was launched by the then Deputy Lord Mayor, Councillor Brendan Brady.

Yet another positive story reported by *Ballymun Concrete News* newsletter. Alas, still without resources, I could not scan or print photographs.

14 February 1999: Yet another powerful story in the *Ballymun Concrete News* newsletter, headlined: "Ballymun Garda Hero Promoted to Detective".

The newsletter report stated:

From my exclusive report in today's Sunday World. *A heroic Garda who helped disarm a crazed gunman at a children's first Holy Communion ceremony in Poppintree last year, has just been promoted through the ranks.*

Garda Joe Everard, based in Ballymun for the past 19 years, goes from a community guard to a detective in the Immigration section at Dublin Airport, just nine months after the tragic event.

The story continued:

The shooting incident, in which Sinn Féin's Larry O'Toole and his son, Larry Junior received gunshot wounds, took place in St Joseph's

Church in Poppintree last May. As angry crowds pounced on the armed gunman, Garda Everard, assisted by Garda Jack Kildea, pulled the gunman from the crowd and Garda Everard took the gun from his possession.

This is another Ballymun, heroic and positive story which, I am happy to say, the national newspaper, the *Sunday World*, also ran.

9 June 1999: The *Ballymun Concrete News* newsletter headline, "Successful Crackdown on Drug Abuse in Ballymun Town Centre".

We reported:

The action taken by Gardaí and security recently, against anti-social behaviour in the Ballymun shopping centre, has yielded tremendous success. New security in the shopping mall, with back up from active Ballymun Gardaí, has finally taken effect. Alleged drug dealing has dramatically dropped in the centre, as Gardaí and security teams escort known drug abusers out of the mall, with little or no resistance.

Garda Inspector Gabriel McIntyre of Santry Garda station said he is pleased with the new security measures and Garda presence in the centre.

"We have the situation under control and we will continue to be active in dealing with crime, from whatever quarter. We are also happy with the current security in the shopping centre. However, we will remain vigilant at all times and our CCTV cameras will record any suspicious activity in the area," he said.

Another powerful Ballymun story with positive results, where drug dealing was cleaned up in the local shopping centre.

These are just a sample of the *Ballymun Concrete News* newsletter positive stories, albeit there are no photographs.

The newsletter served a really good purpose in Ballymun, by providing the area with a much needed, local, independent communication tool. I hope that the stories presented here will show that positive news is not only good for the area, but that positive news can make a difference to the negativity we often see in our lives.

Many of the above stories also appeared in national and regional newspapers, which also demonstrates that national media recognise there is a need for positive, human-interest stories.

Below is a list of issues, dating from 27 July 1998 to December 1998.

- Issue 1. July 27th, 1998. Ballymun Estate Forums and housing task force members asked Environment and Local Government Minister, Noel Dempsey TD, to introduce tax incentives and bring new industry and employment to the area.

- Issue 1. (second edition) July 27th. Hi-Tech Art Centre for Ballymun. A new arts and civic centre, costing £2.2m, is expected to be built in the area within eighteen months.

- Issue 2. July 28th. The Taoiseach, Mr Bertie Ahern TD, launched hi-tech cameras and a Business Watch in the shopping centre to monitor drug abuse.

- Issue 3. July 30th. A special edition and tribute to the late Mrs Pat Mooney R.I.P – a tireless community activist in Ballymun.

- Issue 4. August 5th. "Rock the Blocks Ballymun Style" in the shopping centre.

- Issue 5. August 12th. Chief Superintendent Jim Murphy of Santry Garda station stated how children could be saved from a life of drugs and crime by Juvenile Liaison Officers.

- Issue 6. August 15th. A new vision for scouting in Ballymun through a drug awareness programme.

- Issue 7. August 20th. Brave couple fight tragic illness with faith.

- Issue 8. August 30th. A feature on 'What Are Estate Forums?'.

- Issue 9. September 2nd. Army gives Ballymun residents a lift during lift strike.

- Issue 10. September 11th. Management of lift company and army work together to fix lifts.

- Issue 11. September 24th. Mission Not Impossible for people with disabilities, with Ballymun Active Disability Interest Group. Dublin Corporation Tenants' Charter: the first of its kind in Ireland.

- Issue 12. October 11th. We have the power to change policy. A one-day seminar at Stormanstown House. Seán Ó Cionnaith co-opted on to Dublin City Council.

- Issue 13. October 20th. European Minister, Mr Padraig Flynn's visit to Ballymun Regeneration Ltd.

- Issue 14. November 2nd. Fireworks display on Halloween night. Organised by FAB, Dublin Corporation, local community and Coultry Estate Forum.

- Issue 15. November 22nd. European Drug Prevention week in Ballymun. Ballymun Youth Action Project to host drugs conference at Dublin Castle opened by President Mary McAleese.
- Issue 16. Same week. Torchlight Drug march in Ballymun, ends European Drug Prevention week.
- Issue 17. December 4th. Poppintree man, Aidan Kelly (*Northside People*), edits new book on Finglas.
- Issue 18. December 7th. Sparky, the paralysed terrier dog, to get new wheels for Christmas.
- Issue 19. December 13th. Penthouse raises £11,000 for Senior Citizens. Men's Network treats homeless people to Christmas party.
- Issue 20. December 18th. Winning entries for Dublin Corporation Newsletter Award.
- Issue 21. December 21st. Brave dog, Sparky, gets his new wheels for Christmas.

Chapter 17

My Wife and Family

I cannot finish this book without remembering Kay, my wife of over fifty years and my children, for their major support throughout the lifetime of the newspaper.

Night after night, day after day, week after week, Kay would endure watching me behind the computer, putting the editorial and images together preparing the newspaper for production. I was so engrossed in the work that I hardly had time to drink the cups of tea she would plonk in front of me, on my desk, filled with bundles of paper and office junk.

She would often call me at mealtimes and I would be in the middle of an important phone call, or transcribing notes for stories and I would usually let the dinner get cold. Yes, I was always too busy.

My daughter, Sharon also lived with us and she too had to put up with the annoying sound of me typing away and overusing the only phone, but never complained.

My office, where the newspaper was put together, was a spare room in our three-bedroom flat on the tenth floor of the fifteen-storey Joseph Plunkett Tower. If I was not out chasing stories and gathering advertising for the newspaper, I would, more often than not, be working away in the office in the flat.

This could not have been an ideal situation for my wife, Kay, as I spent most of my time, day and night in my office. Most evenings, she would be sitting, watching TV with my daughter while I was typing away or on the telephone – too busy for even an hour's television. It must have been difficult for Kay and Sharon, but they knew that I had a newspaper to get out and did not have staff to assist me in the process.

I remember the occasions when I returned from the printers with several thousand, freshly printed copies of the newspaper. Both Kay and Sharon got stuck in, helping to pull the heavy bundles into the office. I had to store 20,000 copies of the newspaper in my spare room, as I could not afford to rent premises. So, it was both an office and storeroom.

As I unloaded the newspapers from the back of a friend's van, I had to physically carry them from the van to the lift and up to the tenth floor, where my wife and daughter were ready to carry them to the office. I don't know how my wife put up with the strain of me working tirelessly on the newspaper; she was always patient and supportive of what I was trying to do.

This was important to me. If I did not have her full support, then I could not have possibly carried on running the newspaper. There was no stress on our relationship throughout the newspaper's lifetime; we are both soul mates and were always there for each other. But in the case of running the newspaper, it was Kay who was more there for me.

We often spent long hours into the night, in the early days of the newsletter, stapling the pages together – thousands of four and eight-page newsletters – as I could not afford the additional cost of binding.

When I finalised the proof for the current newspaper and before signing off and sending to printer, I would always run it by Kay, asking her opinion. Kay was not a journalist and no expert in newspaper production, but it was important to me to have her approval.

One of the most important occasions I remember, was the actual official launch of the *Ballymun Concrete News*, with my wife by my side, looking radiant as usual.

The launch took place in the Axis Arts & Community Resource Centre, with over 200 people attending. Not only was I proud of my newspaper but also, having my wife at my side; this showed to all present how much she supported me with the project.

While the newspaper was up and running in the early years, we both enjoyed the buzz of the positive feedback from residents and others. However, when things went wrong, as the newspaper ran into major problems with advertising drying up and even the threat of closure, Kay kept me strong by saying it was others who let me down and not the fault of the newspaper. What she actually meant was that the regeneration failed to deliver the promised major shopping centre and massive investment. She never pointed the finger of blame at me once, as she knew I had poured my all in producing the *Ballymun Concrete News*.

Kay Kelly (wife of *Ballymun Concrete News* editor) at launch of newspaper, 2001.

Kay and daughter, Sharon helped to carry these newspapers into the office on the tenth floor of their Ballymun flat.

Joseph Plunkett Tower in Ballymun. The spare room of Seamus' flat on the tenth floor is where he created and produced the *Ballymun Concrete News*.

Chapter 18

The Right Choice

Looking back now, in my twilight years, at age 74, I often ask myself, did I make the right choices in running my former newspaper?

As I look at my life now, I recognise that I no longer have the energy I once had running the *Concrete News*. Ageing brings its own medical and psychological ailments. I was not immune to this deliberating slowing of the body and mind.

Yes, the loss of my newspaper creation, the *Ballymun Concrete News*, was a crushing blow to myself and my wife. The shock and pain of such a powerful loss was earth shattering and left us bewildered and confused; how and why did my newspaper business crash? Not only the loss of the newspaper but all else that goes with losing a business, especially as a sole trader, which I was.

I was left with debts, which we carried for years but also, the humiliating experience of coming from the prestigious position of an editor-owner of a local newspaper, to being reliant on welfare payments. In addition to the humiliation was the daily pain of explaining to friends, colleagues and especially the people in the community, something which was unexplainable.

It was hard coming face-to-face with people and them asking me, "Where's the *Concrete News*?", not having seen it around anymore. When I did tell them, many of the responses were of shock. After all, they knew through past fund-raising events I had held that I needed help to keep the paper going. However, this time fund raising would not help as, without the planned shopping centre development going ahead, there was no hope of my business surviving.

A lot of local people thought the regeneration company would have saved the paper through investment; that did not happen, however. The newspaper was my responsibility and I alone had to decide to pull the plug as now, without the planned private investment in Ballymun, there was no hope for my business.

So here I am, twelve years on, living with my wife in a nearby area while just a mile up the road from where the old Ballymun flats complex once stood proud, the high-rise tower blocks and apartments have long been flattened, demolished into souvenir pieces of rock.

Right now, in 2018, there is still no shopping centre in Ballymun, the planned massive development, which would have brought thousands of jobs and prosperity to the area and saved my newspaper is no longer a viable option for the Council. Soon, the old, deserted shopping centre will be demolished and that will be the last major landscape icon of Ballymun to disappear from the skyline.

As I look back and recall the earlier memories of the newspaper, I often ask myself, was it worth the pain and sacrifice creating and producing the *Ballymun Concrete News*? Each time, I come up with the same answer: yes, it was well worth the tears and sweat I had invested over eight years running the newspaper. Why? Because I achieved some success in, not only promoting positive news but also, introducing a new concept of news reporting into the press.

This was my dream, to introduce positive news, where negative news was the norm in the mainstream media. I believe that my newspaper and my reporting for the national press achieved this. In addition, as earlier chapters of this book show, there was some serious recognition of my newspaper.

Albeit as a business and a newspaper, it is no longer in production, it still lives through the Dublin City Library digital archives and National Library of Ireland archives, where it will long outlive me and mine, possibly for hundreds of years.

For the *Ballymun Concrete News* in its infancy, the first months and years were tough and challenging but, I decided that I would take on the challenge of running a newspaper with no resources. From my personal point of view, it was worth the risk just to produce a newspaper, which would be the first step in helping to develop a new concept in news reporting.

This was a fresh and positive way of presenting the news, which broke the mould of negative, stereotypical style reporting. It was more positive, rock-solid, professional news, promoting the good in an area, which was incorrectly labelled disadvantaged and not a nice place to live or invest. I believe my newspaper proved the very opposite, that not only was Ballymun a good place to live and invest but the area had a really close-knit community of people working together.

Eleven years on, the high-rise flats complex is now replaced with houses and apartments and a mixture of small, local retail shops and neighbourhood centres. However, it still lacks a heart – a shopping centre, which brings with it, more interaction within a community.

I know, from my own experience, an independent newspaper as a business would not survive in an area with little or no retail advertising to cover production costs. Perhaps that's why, in eleven years, no attempt was made to introduce another newspaper in the area. However, I strongly believe that Ballymun needs its own independent newspaper to cover and report local news stories.

As I said, I am too old now, even if there were an opportunity to start a newspaper. If, however, a local newspaper with the *Ballymun Concrete News* ethos and mission statement of Positive News Only was offered, I would gladly offer training to any potential editor. Yet again, because of lack of advertising and commercial viability, it's very unlikely that a newspaper would survive, unless there was substantially more private investment in the area. I am still reeling over the loss of my newspaper; I don't suppose I will ever really get over its sudden demise. Ballymun still needs a newspaper and I feel useless that I can do nothing about it.

There is still considerable unease and uncertainty in Ballymun, as there's no real communication tool to inform residents what is happening in the area. That was my role for eight years: keeping local residents up to date with all the news and developments in the area. Now, they have to rely on social media, neighbours, friends, local gossip and whatever Ballymun news I can provide, with the voluntary help from a reporter friend, through my Facebook pages. Although I do my best to keep residents informed, the Facebook pages will never be a substitute for the *Concrete News*, or another real Ballymun newspaper.

I can only hope that another professional journalist, with a good knowledge of the area, its recent history and the necessary resources, will at least set up a Ballymun newsletter, as I did in 1997. Even a regular, one-page news-sheet produced by a journalist can keep residents informed of the latest local developments. I think such a person can learn from my experience in creating the *Ballymun Concrete News*, that it's not impossible to run a voluntary, professional, one-page newsletter in the area and gradually build on that. It may not be a newspaper like the *Concrete News* but, it can still be a communication tool, delivering factual, balanced news to fill a void.

I hope this book will inspire some up-and-coming young journalist to start up a one-page news-sheet and produce it on a voluntary basis, as there is no viable advertising in the area to support a newspaper. All I can say, at this point, is that I did all that was humanly possible to keep the *Ballymun*

Concrete News in operation but, without the promised shopping centre and private investment in Ballymun, it was useless to even try without revenue to count on.

I don't have any regrets in setting up and producing the *Ballymun Concrete News*. I feel, through my newspaper, I have shown there's a new way of reporting news that helps communities like Ballymun. Through regular positive news reporting, any deprived area that is labelled-disadvantaged can only benefit from the reporting it rightly deserves.

Chapter 19

The Rock-Solid, Positive Way Forward for the Press Media

Over the lifetime of the *Ballymun Concrete News* and my reporting of positive news in these publications, I believe this has shown that rock-solid, positive news reporting is up to same standard as other major national news stories and are received well in national and regional newspapers. It is not only effective but generates good feelings among readers. While negative-headlined front-page stories seem to be the template for many tabloid newspapers, I believe there is a growing need for more positive, good news stories, as readers become almost immune to the constant stream of negative stereotyping flowing from these type of news headlines.

The feedback that I received from my readers in relation to my positive news reports in national press and the *Ballymun Concrete News*, has proven to me that people want a change, from the negative style to the rock-solid, positive news headline reporting. The future of news reporting, I believe, needs to be more focused on what's good in the world, in addition to the inevitable negative stories. Each has to be reported – both the good and the bad news – but there needs to be a balance of good and bad (negative and positive) reported on, especially on the front pages of national and regional newspapers.

From my experience of reporting in the *Ballymun Concrete News*, as well as national and regional newspapers, I have found that you can write a story in a sensational way to attract readers, accompanied by a good headline and photograph. This is the way newspapers sell, through sensational headlines and striking photographs and images, to encourage people to pick up and purchase the newspaper (as the saying goes, 'Headlines sells newspapers'). With reports of newspaper sales falling and the online news and social media filling a void (a hunger for a different type of news), the newspaper industry and its journalists face a bleak future, if this trend continues.

When I see, on one of my public Facebook pages (Ballymun Talks) the different type of conversations taking place (good and bad) overall, there is an overwhelming evidence of goodwill, glowing from most posts and comments. The most recent being the public response to the fire at the nearby Metro Hotel in Ballymun. Within a few short hours, offers of help of clothing for residents and guests of the hotel apartments were being posted on the Facebook page. There was a huge number of comments on the page, offering to help in one way or another. This was a Ballymun community in positive mode, helping others. This is just one part of social media, which shows how people react to situations in a very positive way.

The Metro Hotel story, reported in all media, was not a negative one, as the guests and residents were all rescued and the fire was under control within hours. However, the response of the local community on social media was heart-warming. This is an example how people, as in Ballymun, react to the way stories of tragic events and heroism are reported. Tragedies, in this sense of the word, are not negative, as all survived the fire, which gutted three floors of the high-rise hotel apartment block. As I said before, there is a major difference between a negative story and a tragedy. The tragedy is more of a human-interest story, reflecting the hurt caused to the victims of such events. These type of stories, as in Ballymun's Metro Hotel, tend to bring out the best in people, who instinctively react in a very human way, with offers of assistance and aid.

This was also duplicated in the London Grenfell fire, a major tragedy but a massive reaction from, not only the community but the world at large, responding via the social media with huge offers of help to survivors of the fire. Once again, people reacted positively to a very human-interest story. The news of the victims being killed in the fire and the survivors who had their own story to tell, touched people's hearts. They, in turn, responded in a natural, generous, human way. This is what news reporting is all about: telling positive, human-interest stories, which reach the hearts of their reader and not bombard them with savage events such as murder, crime and other such horror stories on the front pages.

People need a newspaper which, not only report positive news but also create a template for this type of news, as they already have for the negative, gory news. This type of positive news needs to be continuous and become almost routine daily reporting. There is a need for positive, human-interest stories to be published on front pages and other negative-type reports on inside pages. More exposure of readers to good, rock-solid stories on the front page and near front pages (like the above-mentioned reaction to tragedies) brings out the best in people and also creates a feel-good factor.

When I took the risk in producing rock-solid, positive news in the *Ballymun Concrete News*, as well as national and regional newspapers, people responded positively in turn. I increased the circulation of the *Ballymun Concrete News* from 7,500 copies per monthly issue to 20,000 in less than two years, because of its popular style of reporting and colourful production.

My newspaper reports in national press ranged in volume, from a single column to front page and two-page spread exclusives over an almost 20-year period. This showed the success in reporting positive and human-interest stories both at national and local level.

Will the press change its editorial stance from the template of negative, front-page, gory reports to more rock-solid positive and human-interest stories? I don't think they will in the foreseeable future. I think that there is a train of thought among media moguls that, 'If it's not broken, don't fix it'. That is a mistake, in my opinion. It may not be broken but it is suffering from drops in sales, the effects of internet, social media, latest news online with up to the minute reports. The constant barrage of front-page, gory, negative news headlines and stories only contributes to this.

It is a simple turnaround from the negative to the positive, as I have shown with my newspaper and my published reports over the years. There would be a dramatic increase in sales if more positive front-page headlines were employed. The increased advertising that this would give rise to would also yield more jobs for freelance and staff journalists.

Surely, a major union, such as the NUJ (National Union of Journalists) can see the writing on the walls for its journalist members if the current downward trend in sales continues. There is power in a union of journalists, who provide the stories for newspapers, both in reporting and production. Such a movement can influence change of direction of the newspaper industry, from the current negative editorial to a more balanced, rock-solid positive, in-your-face images and news.

The way forward for the newspaper industry is to focus on what people really want to read. Do they want to continue reading the daily tabloid front-page headlines with graphic images of drug lords, murders, terrorists, rapists and others who are criminally orientated? Or, do they want to read, on their front page, the good news stories and pictures of people being rescued when disaster strikes, stories of heroism – the kind of stories that pull at readers' heartstrings and encourage them to purchase newspapers? That is the burning question newspaper moguls want to ask themselves – how to put the readers first in the process rather than the blind pursuit of profits. The idea of 'people before profit' needs to be at the forefront of any newspaper business or empire.

Readers, in my opinion, want honesty from their newspapers and not made-up stories from well-written press releases, often coming from major advertisers. Steer clear from running stories copied from social media tweets and Facebook pages. These are not reliable sources of information.

Boots on the ground, face-to-face journalism is the only way to get accurate reporting and news.

Because we live in an internet age, its only too easy to copy from the web pages and social media, knowing that's not a reliable source and yet, use it as news. Is a tweet from an American president or major celebrity news? That is what's happening: suddenly, a tweet or Facebook messages becomes a major story. What's happened to investigative reporting? Getting reporters out there, following up leads that uncover a major story. It is becoming a rarity these days, with the odd exception of television current affairs programmes.

Readers love to read stories of politicians, bankers and powerful figures caught out in the act of corruption. This is, in mine and readers' eyes, good, positive news – catching corrupt, powerful, white-collared criminals. This is what they want to read. I've often heard it said, the day after a TV prime time current affairs programme uncovers political or white-collared crime, "God, did you see that programme last night? It was great. It's about time, someone exposed these people for who they really are."

So, it's not about someone's tweets on social media or Facebook messages. That's just not news. It is, in my opinion, a cheap shot at journalism and brings disrepute to the profession.

This brings us back to what positive news really is. The mission statement of my newspaper was to produce positive news only, in a locally disadvantaged community, who had experienced mainly negative news for almost forty years. For other similar socially disadvantaged areas like Ballymun, it can be a real problem to have newspapers reporting only negative news about their particular areas. These negative stories can only destroy the image of the area, creating more unemployment arising from less investment into the community.

The 21st century, is a time to reflect on what type of news we want from our newspapers. Do we want a press that only wants to push criminality, murders, drug lords and other gangland crimes in your face when you go to pick up a newspaper and see these images on the front page? Or, do we want to see more positive stories, that speak of bravery, heroism, life-saving acts and other stories that reflect good events and acts in our community, city or country.

At the end of the day, it's really down to the general public what they want to read and purchase. Will they stop buying the negative, stereotyping tabloid newspapers or just get what news they want to read online, social media or that being broadcast on radio or television?

Newspaper industry, start to rethink your editorial and listen to what the public are saying. Do not be too focused on profits from major advertisers.

Positive news is the way forward. Let the headlines reflect what the newspaper is really about: respect for its readers, common decency, enabling the reader to feel good after reading your newspaper.

I have written this book, not only to relate my own journey and the story that has unravelled but also, in the hope that it might influence a new concept in journalism – that of producing Rock-Solid, Positive News. Hopefully, as a concept, it will grow and become so engrained until the point is reached that, as the title suggests, it's written in concrete.

Summary

Through my experience of running the *Ballymun Concrete News* and also reporting for the national newspapers, I have found there is a need for more newspapers, such as the *Ballymun Concrete News*, to counteract the negative news headlined in sections of the press.

If the country had numerous similar newspapers that kept to a Positive News Only ethos, just think of the benefits that would flow to each community and to the country as a whole.

While there is a constant stream of negative press in almost every media outlet in the country, a balance needs to be struck between negative and positive news. It is my belief that people are sickened by the sensational type of negative news, which hits them with the early morning papers at the breakfast table.

This current trend towards excessive reporting of negative news is not going to change overnight, as this type of news has become embedded in newspaper editorial thinking. So, unless there is more focus on creating and developing different types of news, to attract a larger readership in the press, the industry faces collapse.

From my own experience with the *Ballymun Concrete News*, I have found that positive news creates an atmosphere of good feelings, since people love reading about the happy events in their communities. Having talked to people about the news content of the *Ballymun Concrete News*, there was a general consensus that this type of news was not only different but more enjoyable to read. (These views are also supported by a number of academics and journalists).

My hope now, is that newspapers like the *Ballymun Concrete News* might begin to spring up in other communities. Back in 1997, it was my dream to create such a newspaper and I am proud to say that this dream came through, albeit after a wait of a few years. I now have another dream that, in the years to come, the *Ballymun Concrete News* style of editorial will be duplicated in other newspapers all over the country.

Just imagine the effects that this type of news will have on a tired people, being subjected to negative, sensationalised news round the clock for 52 weeks a year. As you visualise readers looking at the front pages, with graphic headlines and stories containing images of gory murders, suicides, terrorists, images of bloodied bodies in war-torn cities, just imagine what effect the alternative could have on readers.

Presently, there would seem to be no let up of negative news, which is bound to affect all who are constantly exposed to it. From my experience, as a former national press journalist, I know just how it affected me. It is not a very nice experience seeing these images constantly. What effects do they have on very sensitive people who read what, in most cases I would describe as horror stories? Would they lead to depression anxiety, nervous breakdowns or even copycat syndrome?

All newspaper editors need to think long and hard about the effects the hard-core negative news has on these people. Most people live with enough of their own personal and domestic problems, without having to carry the negative world, as conveyed by newspapers, on their shoulders as well. Yes, the stories may be real and they are news but, their presentation in such a graphic and negative editorial can be avoided with thoughtful planning.

The *Ballymun Concrete News*, as a newspaper, tried to redress the balance between negative and positive news in the Ballymun community. This may seem small in comparison to national news but, Ballymun featured regularly in national newspapers because of its high-rise, concrete, graffiti-vandalised and council-maintenance-neglected flats were an attraction to news media looking to portray a negative image. No matter what crimes occurred in Ballymun, they automatically became a national story, as the run-down estate, in itself, created a negative stereotype for news editors to exploit. The Ballymun high-rise skyline has, over the past forty years, became a newspaper attraction, focusing mainly on the negative aspect of the lives of its 17,000-plus residents.

In some ways, the media's continuous negative focus on the Ballymun area helped to give its undeserved label. However, it was the *Ballymun Concrete News* which reversed the negativity and showed the Ballymun area as a close-knit and positive community.

As the editor of the *Ballymun Concrete News* and a Ballymun resident, I knew that there were hundreds (if not thousands) of positive stories and activity in the area, which needed reporting. And as the press were not familiar, or not interested in these, I felt it my duty to ensure that many of these great stories would be published in my own newspaper.

In addition to my own newspaper reports, I ensured that some of these same stories would not go unnoticed by the national press. That is why

I submitted them to the national newspapers. However, as most of my time was dedicated to running the *Ballymun Concrete News*, it was more important to report the positive stories locally, as they would then get the coverage they merited, something they may not receive in a national newspaper.

The thousands of events and stories I have covered over the years, as a journalist, have taught me that, while people are important, communities are equally important. And it has always been the mission of the *Ballymun Concrete News* to highlight positive news and events in the Ballymun community, which I believed the paper has succeeded in doing.

I believe I have always put the community first and I have learned much from the positive and exciting news stories that I covered. With over 100 plus voluntary community groups active in the area over the years, there was never a shortage of such stories.

There has also been a share of human-interest stories and features that the *Ballymun Concrete News* was honoured to publish, even if they were often sad stories.

Then, of course, there was the *Ballymun Concrete News* record of the regeneration of Ballymun, where the high-rise complex was demolished and replaced with new housing and infrastructure.

These and the thousands of stories that I have covered and photographed in Ballymun, have not only been educational but, it has been an honour, for me personally, to have been the editor who decided upon such positively themed stories

Appendix

Links to websites and resources referenced in this book

Ballymun Concrete News – the complete newspaper archive is available from Dublin City Library and Archive (see below) in digital format while the National Library of Ireland (see below) holds the hard copies which are available to view by appointment.

Ballymun Concrete News 1 (Facebook page) – www.facebook.com/ballymunconcretenews1/

Ballymun Concrete News Photo Archive (Facebook page) – www.facebook.com/ballymunconcretenewsphotoarchive/

Ballymun Talks (Facebook public group) – www.facebook.com/groups/240368176360323

Dublin Concrete News (Facebook page) – www.facebook.com/dublinconcretenews/

Dublin City Library and Archive – www.dublincity.ie/ballymun-concrete-news

Irish Examiner 3 August 2005:
Ballymun; From High Hopes to Broken Dreams by Seamus Kelly and Tom Farrell – www.irishexaminer.com/ireland/ballymun-from-high-hopes-to-broken-dreams-345936.html

National Library of Ireland – catalogue.nli.ie/Record/vtls000171559

National Union of Journalists (NUJ) code of conduct – www.nuj.org.uk/about/nuj-code/